THE BRITISH WOMEN'S SUFFRAGE CAMPAIGN, 1866–1928

THE BRITISH WOMEN'S SUFFRAGE CAMPAIGN, 1866–1928

HAROLD L. SMITH

LONGMAN
LONDON AND NEW YORK

Addison Wesley Longman Limited
Edinburgh Gate
Harlow
Essex CM20 2JE
United Kingdom
and Associated Companies throughout the world

Published in the United States of America
by Addison Wesley Longman, New York

© Addison Wesley Longman Limited 1998

First published 1998

ISBN 0 582 298113

Visit Addison Wesley Longman on the world wide web at http://www.awl-he.com

British Library Cataloguing-in-Publication Data

A catalogue record for this book is available from the British Library

Library of Congress Cataloging-in-Publication Data

Smith, Harold L.
     The British women's suffrage campaign, 1866–1928 / Harold L.
Smith
          p.   cm. -- (Seminar studies in history)
     Includes bibliographical references (p.   ) and index.
     ISBN 0-582-29811-3
     1. Women's movement--Great Britain--History. 2. Women--Suffrage-
-Great Britain--History. 3. Women in politics--Great Britain-
-History. I. Title. II. Series.
HQ1236.5.G3S55 1998
305.42'0941--dc21   98-4025
                                                                            CIP

Set by 7
Printed in Malaysia, PP

CONTENTS

AN INTRODUCTION TO THE SERIES

Such is the pace of historical enquiry in the modern world that there is an ever-widening gap between the specialist article or monograph, incorporating the results of current research, and general surveys, which inevitably become out of date. *Seminar Studies in History* are designed to bridge this gap. The series was founded by Patrick Richardson in 1966 and his aim was to cover major themes in British, European and World history. Between 1980 and 1996 Roger Lockyer continued his work, before handing the editorship over to Clive Emsley and Gordon Martel. Clive Emsley is Professor of History at the Open University, while Gordon Martel is Professor of International History at the University of Northern British Columbia, Canada and Senior Research Fellow at De Montfort University.

All the books are written by experts in their field who are not only familiar with the latest research but have often contributed to it. They are frequently revised, in order to take account of new information and interpretations. They provide a selection of documents to illustrate major themes and provoke discussion, and also a guide to further reading. The aim of *Seminar Studies* is to clarify complex issues without over-simplifying them, and to stimulate readers into deepening their knowledge and understanding of major themes and topics.

NOTE ON REFERENCING SYSTEM

Readers should note that numbers in square brackets [5] refer them to the corresponding entry in the Bibliography at the end of the book (specific page references are given in italic). A number in square brackets preceded by *Doc.* [*Doc. 5*] refers readers to the corresponding item in the Document section which follows the main text. Words and abbreviations asterisked at first occurrence are defined in the Glossary.

ABBREVIATIONS

CUWFA	Conservative and Unionist Women's Franchise Association
CWSS	Catholic Women's Suffrage Society
EFF	Election Fighting Fund Committee
ELF	East London Federation of the Women's Social and Political Union (later of the Suffragettes)
EPRDC	Equal Political Rights Demonstration Committee
ILP	Independent Labour Party
IWSA	International Women's Suffrage Alliance
LSWS	London Society for Women's Suffrage (later London Society for Women's Service)
NEC	National Executive Committee (of the Labour Party)
NESWS	North of England Society for Women's Suffrage
NSWS	National Society for Women's Suffrage
NUSEC	National Union of Societies for Equal Citizenship
NUWSS	National Union of Women's Suffrage Societies
PSF	People's Suffrage Federation
SJCIWO	Standing Joint Committee of Industrial Women's Organizations
WCG	Women's Co-operative Guild
WFL	Women's Freedom League
WLF	Women's Liberal Federation
WNAL	Women's National Anti-Suffrage League
WSPU	Women's Social and Political Union

ACKNOWLEDGEMENTS

This book is dedicated to Judy.

I would like to thank David Doughan, Fawcett Reference Librarian, for his assistance above and beyond the call of duty. Special thanks are due to Philippa Levine for reading and commenting on Chapter one. I would like to thank the University of Houston-Victoria Academic Council for financial support which made a research trip to Great Britain possible. But above all, I would like to thank my life-partner and in-house editor: Judith N. McArthur.

PUBLISHER'S ACKNOWLEDGEMENTS

The publishers would like to thank the following for permission to reproduce copyright material:

Dr Barbara S. McCrimmon for The First Suffrage Petition from Helen Taylor to Barbara Bodichon; Routledge Publishers for an extract from *Suffrage and the Pankhursts*, edited by J. Marcus pp. 188-9, 194 and 234 published in 1987; The House of Lords Record Office on behalf of the Beaverbrook Trustees for an extract from 'Women's Suffrage Deputation March 29 1917', Lloyd George Papers, F/229/3.

Whilst every effort has been made to trace the owners of copyright material, in a few cases this has proved to be problematic and so we take this opportunity to offer our apologies to any holders whose rights we may have unwittingly infringed.

FOREWORD

In terms of its stated objective, the women's suffrage campaign was a success story: the principle of women's suffrage was conceded in 1918 and equal franchise rights followed in 1928. The campaign brought into being Britain's largest women's mass movement, and heightened expectations of gender reform. But by the time equal franchise was obtained, reformers were already becoming disillusioned with parliamentary politics. From the beginning of the campaign, many women had wanted something more than just equal access to a male-controlled political system; they wished to change the system to reflect women's values. By 1928 it had become apparent that this vision of a radical transformation of gender structures would not be achieved in the near future, and that equal franchise merely meant the opportunity to participate in a male-dominated political system. This book attempts to explain how this came about.

Ray Strachey's study, *The Cause* (1928) [28], was the first serious attempt to write the history of the women's suffrage campaign, but its Whiggish account of the inevitable triumph of a just cause did not capture the public imagination (nor that of historians) to the extent that Sylvia Pankhurst's *The Suffragette Movement* did when it appeared in 1931. Pankhurst's book probably did more than any other volume to shape interpretations of the suffrage campaign for the next 30 years: the Women's Social and Political Union (WSPU) was at the centre of the story and within it the Pankhurst family were the central characters. As late as the 1970s, when the BBC prepared a documentary on the women's suffrage campaign, it (and the accompanying book, *Shoulder to Shoulder*, by Midge Mackenzie) concentrated on the WSPU and the Pankhursts.

The historiography of the women's suffrage movement has undergone a dramatic transformation in the past two decades. The publication of Sandra Stanley Holton's *Feminism and Democracy: Women's Suffrage and Reform Politics in Britain 1900–1918* [58] in 1986 was a turning-point. The use of new archival material by Holton, Jo Vellacott, Leslie Hume and David Rubenstein has altered our understanding of the National Union of Women's Suffrage Societies (NUWSS) and its contribution to franchise reform. Holton and Liz Stanley have enabled us to see that there was much more to the WSPU than the Pankhursts, and, with Martha Vicinus, to view it as part of a gender revolt against traditional sex roles rather than being narrowly concerned with the franchise.

There have been many studies of the British women's suffrage campaign in the period prior to 1914, but this is the first which traces it from its beginnings in the 1860s to its successful conclusion in 1928. Although I have drawn upon my own research where relevant, especially in the chapter on the 1920s, this is primarily a work of synthesis. All students of the women's suffrage movement are deeply in debt to Sandra Holton, Martin Pugh, Philippa Levine, Brian Harrison, Angela John, Jo Vellacott and many others whose pioneering studies have made this attempt at synthesis possible. In order to keep this book within the length set by the publisher, I have had to prune rigorously and, in some instances, even delete topics which deserved inclusion. I would hope that readers will consider this volume the starting-point of their investigation into the women's suffrage movement rather than the end.

PART ONE: THE CAMPAIGN

1 THE VICTORIAN SUFFRAGE CAMPAIGN, 1866–1897

Earlier accounts of the women's suffrage campaign portrayed it as part of the nineteenth-century movement for a more democratic franchise which also sought to extend the suffrage to disenfranchised men. While acknowledging this connection, the campaign is now viewed as part of a specifically women's protest against female oppression. Women did not seek the vote solely to gain equal citizenship rights, but as a means to the political power necessary to transform gender structures. Accompanying this changed perspective has been a shift in the relationship between the suffrage campaign and other women's reform movements. While earlier studies considered the suffrage campaign to be separate from other Victorian female reform movements, it is now regarded as part of a broader reform impulse seeking to eliminate restrictions on women's educational and employment opportunities, gendered pay scales, the sexual double standard and the legal authority husbands held over their wives [76, 61].

ORIGINS

Women's suffrage became a matter of public concern during the early nineteenth-century discussion of franchise reform. In response to James Mill's claim in 1820 that there was no need to extend the suffrage to women because their fathers and husbands would protect their interests, William Thompson and Anna Wheeler presented a case for women's right to vote in *An Appeal of One Half the Human Race . . .* [30]. In the debate on the 1832 Reform Bill, Henry Hunt introduced a petition to grant the vote to unmarried women who met the bill's property requirements. Parliament responded by passing legislation which for the first time explicitly restricted the suffrage to men; the Reform Act specified that it enfranchised 'male persons'.

During the following decades there were several attempts to revive the issue. The Chartist movement included women in the 1838 People's Charter, although later versions changed the demand to adult male suffrage. In 1851 Anne Knight, a Quaker and anti-slavery campaigner, assisted Chartist women in establishing the Sheffield Female Political Association which drafted the women's suffrage petition introduced in the House of Lords later that year [97].

The organized women's movement originated with a group of women who met at Langham Place in London in the 1850s and 1860s. Led by Barbara Leigh Smith Bodichon and Bessie Rayner Parkes, it became an important source of proposals for gender reform in education, employment and politics which they conveyed to a wider audience through their periodical, the *English Woman's Journal* [76]. Members of this group established the Married Women's Property Committee in 1855 that successfully pressed for reform of the law in order to grant married women property rights [56]. The *English Woman's Journal* encouraged interest in women's suffrage by printing articles on it in the 1860s. Women from the Langham Place circle were prominent in the Kensington Society, a debating group formed in 1865, which advocated women's suffrage among other reforms; it later became the London Society for Women's Suffrage.

An organized women's suffrage movement emerged when a new reform bill became a possibility in the mid-1860s. John Stuart Mill included women's suffrage in his election programme when he was elected to parliament in 1865. At Bodichon's request, Mill agreed to introduce a women's suffrage amendment if the women's groups would prepare a petition [*Doc. 1*]. Suffrage societies were quickly formed in London and Manchester; Mill presented their petition with 1,499 signatures to parliament in 1866. When Disraeli's 1867 Reform Bill was considered by the House of Commons, Mill proposed substituting the term 'person' for 'man', but his amendment was rejected by a vote of 194 to 73.

During the 1860s suffragists often based their claim for the vote on the grounds that women had been allowed to vote in the past, and that in 1850 Lord Brougham's Act specified that the term 'man' in all legislation was to be taken as including women unless it expressly excluded them. On this basis Lydia Becker encouraged women who met the 1867 Reform Act's property qualifications to attempt to register to vote. In November 1868 this view was rejected by the Court of Common Pleas in the Chorlton v. Lings decision, thus forcing the suffrage movement to seek legislation granting women the vote [61].

Ray Strachey's portrayal of the Victorian suffrage campaign as a London-based movement, dominated by moderate women drawn from the social elite, has been revised by recent studies [28]. Sandra Holton finds the roots of the women's suffrage movement in mid-nineteenth-century northern radicalism, and stresses the continuity between it and the Edwardian militant suffrage movement [61]. The women who initiated the women's suffrage movement tended to be religious dissenters, often Unitarian or Quaker, to have been active in radical political groups such as the Manchester-based Anti-Corn Law League or the anti-slavery movement, and to have connections with male radicals seeking a more democratic franchise [61].

Strachey presented the suffrage campaign as a socially conservative movement of respectable ladies by separating it from the reform efforts concerned with sexuality. Judith Walkowitz, however, considers the demand for the vote to have been fuelled by women's growing outrage against the sexual double standard [115]. The 1864 Contagious Diseases Act (extended in 1866 and 1869) required women suspected by the police of being prostitutes to have a medical examination to determine if they had venereal disease. Women were outraged by this for several reasons. The Acts did not require that men be examined, thus implying that women were solely responsible for spreading venereal diseases. It deprived women of civil liberties, since a woman could be suspected of prostitution merely by walking in certain sections of a town. Finally, the legislation applied only to towns with military bases and seemed designed to protect the sexual double standard by enabling men to frequent prostitutes without fear of disease. The Acts thus seemed a blatant example of the tendency of an all-male parliament elected solely by male voters to legislate in men's interests at women's expense.

Recent writing has also shifted attention away from the London Society to the more radical Manchester Society. The latter was established by Elizabeth Wolstenholme in 1866, prior to the formation of the London Society, and it became the dominant suffrage organization in the early years of the campaign. Following the creation of suffrage societies in Edinburgh, Bristol and Birmingham, it was the Manchester Society which in 1867 was responsible for bringing the local suffrage groups together in the National Society for Women's Suffrage (NSWS)*, a loose federation intended to facilitate joint action for reform [61].

Strachey's depiction of the suffrage leaders as conservatives is also misleading. Radical suffragists played key roles in the Manchester Society from the beginning. Wolstonholme, the society's first secretary, was notorious for her advanced feminism. Ursula Bright and her husband, Jacob, (the younger brother of John Bright), were prominent members, while Richard Pankhurst, a radical lawyer, joined shortly after it was formed. Pankhurst drafted the first women's suffrage bill which Jacob Bright introduced in parliament in 1870.

Further evidence of the Manchester Society's importance is suggested by the fact that its secretary, Lydia Becker, was the suffrage campaign's first national secretary.* Originally part of the Manchester Radical group, Becker was active in the campaign against the Contagious Diseases Acts in the 1860s and was a member of the Married Women's Property Committee until 1873. She founded the *Women's Suffrage Journal* in 1870, and edited it until her death in 1890. She became the NSWS's parliamentary secretary shortly after it was formed and directed the parliamentary campaign during the following decades.

The women who established the suffrage organizations in the 1860s were not political neophytes. Some had participated in the anti-slavery campaign while others had been active in the Anti-Corn Law League. Suffragists drew upon their experience with these pressure groups in choosing to organize on a non-party basis and in relying on private members' bills which could be supported by back-benchers from all parties. While this approach had worked for pressure groups earlier in the century, the increased role of the political party in late-Victorian Britain made it less effective. Brian Harrison considers this strategy to have been a major reason for the failure to achieve reform prior to 1914 [54].

Success in securing the vote in local elections encouraged reformers to anticipate an early concession of the parliamentary franchise. Jacob Bright's amendment to the 1869 Municipal Corporations (Franchise) Act granted women the right to vote in local elections on the same basis as men. This enfranchised single women ratepayers; a married woman normally could not vote because her husband was legally the ratepayer [57]. It set a precedent that led to women being granted the right to vote for the local school boards established by the 1870 Education Act. By 1892 there were 503,000 women eligible to vote in local elections in England, Scotland and Wales; they would have comprised at least 10 per cent of the parliamentary electorate if women had been permitted to vote in national elections with the same qualifications [91].

IDEOLOGY

The belief that the women's suffrage movement's ideology was based on liberal equal rights doctrine has been replaced by a more complex interpretation. Although some women did use equal rights language derived from liberalism, many did not. Some women rejected equal rights ideology because it implied that women wished to have the rights men did, and, by implication, to become more like men. Rather than minimize sexual difference as equal rights advocates did, they celebrated difference in order to encourage a sense of pride in female identity [*Doc. 2*]. Instead of rejecting a separate spheres ideology, they turned its notion of female moral superiority into a justification for women's suffrage. If the family benefited from women's purity, then bringing women into the public sphere should elevate the moral tone of public life too. This sense of female moral superiority linked the suffrage movement to other female reform movements explicitly concerned with sexuality, such as the late-nineteenth-century purity campaign [38].

Female suffragists used a variety of arguments for reform. Partly because the 1867 Reform Act had reinforced the connection between property ownership and enfranchisement, reformers stressed that females were the only group of tax-paying property owners denied the right to vote for their representatives [*Doc. 3*]. This effectively cut through the smoke screen of anti-suffrage arguments to the crucial point: suffrage was a gender issue which was resisted because it would grant women the power to undermine existing gender structures which worked to their disadvantage. Given the undeniable fact that the franchise was based on a property qualification, and that some women met the property requirement, suffrage opponents resorted to claims that voting was unfeminine and inconsistent with a woman's nature [100].

Although gender-based disabilities, such as exclusion from the franchise, encouraged women to view each other as members of a sex-class, they were divided by party affiliation, social class, religion, and political outlook. From the beginning conservatives and radicals found it difficult to work with each other. In the 1860s Emily Davies had been reluctant to help launch a public campaign for women's suffrage for fear it would attract 'wild people' [women] who 'would insist on jumping like kangaroos . . . ' [*38 p. 84*]. Davies and Frances Power Cobbe, both Conservatives, became members of the London Society's Executive Committee in the 1860s, but both resigned after a brief period because they disliked the committee's radical women [38].

Suffragists were also divided over the role of men in the suffrage movement. When the Provisional Committee that became the London Society* was being formed, Helen Taylor opposed allowing men to join. Bodichon, supported by Clementia Taylor, objected that this would delay obtaining the vote since men's co-operation would be necessary for reform. Men were included on the committee, but Helen Taylor continued to press the issue and men were excluded from the London Society's 'managing committee' (executive) when it replaced the Provisional Committee the following year [56]. Elsewhere men were usually welcomed; suffragists considered their participation in mixed organizations an improvement over the early Victorian practice of relegating women to female auxiliaries in reform organizations [34].

DISPUTES WITHIN THE MOVEMENT

In 1871 the suffrage movement underwent the first of three major splits (the others followed in 1888 and 1915). The 1871 division arose over the relationship between the suffrage organization and the campaign to repeal the Contagious Diseases Acts directed by the Ladies' National Association for the Repeal of the Contagious Diseases Acts (LNA). Although suffragists generally opposed the Acts, many shared Millicent Fawcett's fear that public support for repealing the Acts would discredit the suffrage movement and therefore refused to be associated with the repeal campaign. But seventeen prominent suffragists, including the founders of suffrage societies in Edinburgh, Bristol, and Manchester considered repeal so important to women that they joined the LNA executive [115].

In the midst of this dispute the Manchester Society initiated a change in the National Society that increased the power of the provincial organizations relative to the one in London. Late in 1871 a Central Committee was established, chaired by Jacob Bright, the Manchester Society's leader. The London Society opposed this change, and refused to join the new Central Committee. The London Society itself then divided; those who believed the organized suffrage movement should not support the CD repeal campaign, such as Millicent Fawcett,* retained control. The London Society then withdrew from the National Society until 1877. In addition to revealing the strong differences of opinion between radical and conservative suffragists, the split weakened the pressure for women's suffrage bills during the early 1870s when parliament gave serious consideration to reform [61].

Suffragists were divided from the beginning by the problem of how to formulate their demand. The critical issue was whether to include married women. Under the legal doctrine of coverture a married woman had no separate legal identity from her husband, and thus could not own real property. Since property ownership was required for the right to vote, proposing that women be granted the vote on the same terms as men would exclude married women.

Influenced by Conservative women such as Emily Davies and Frances Power Cobbe, the London Society initially proposed that the vote be given only to women who had *femme sole* status – unmarried women and widows. The Manchester Society, however, reflecting the more radical views of the Bright circle, urged that married women be included in the demand. A compromise was eventually agreed upon which demanded the vote for women on the same terms as men. Since men's right to vote was based on the property qualification, this in effect excluded married women, but as it did not explicitly do so they could be included later if the property qualification was removed.

LEGISLATION PROPOSED

Jacob Bright became the movement's parliamentary leader after Mill was defeated in the 1868 election, and introduced the first women's suffrage bill in 1870. It proposed that women be given the vote on the same terms as men, thus embodying the compromise formula which reflected the principle of sex equality. It passed its second reading with a 33 vote majority, but was defeated in the committee stage when the Prime Minister, William Gladstone, made it an issue of party loyalty by declaring his opposition.

Although suffrage bills were introduced almost every year during the 1870s, the best opportunity for reform came when the Liberal Government's 1884 Reform Bill was under consideration. In order to make it acceptable to as many MPs as possible, the women's suffrage amendment to the bill was narrowly drawn; it would have enfranchised only about 100,000 women, most of them well-to-do property owners. The amendment drew considerable Conservative support since most of the proposed women voters were expected to vote Tory. This would have partially offset the bill's enfranchisement of male rural labourers, most of whom were Liberals. But when Gladstone announced his opposition 104 MPs who had declared themselves supporters of reform voted against it, thereby causing the amendment to be rejected by a vote of 271 to 135 [61].

Suffragists were demoralized by the 1884 defeat because they erroneously believed it completed the extension of the franchise to men, and thus expected parliament's interest in franchise reform to end. Upper- and middle-class women also resented the Act's implication that masculinity was valued more highly than class position. Elite women felt that enfranchising agricultural labourers, while denying the vote to the lady of the manor, undermined the social hierarchy at their expense [100]. Frances Power Cobbe was incensed that 'a rabble of illiterates' should have been enfranchised while educated women, their social superiors, were denied the vote [77 *p. 61*].

The fate of the 1884 suffrage amendment suggests why the Victorian reform movement was unsuccessful. The majority of the MPs supporting women's suffrage were Liberals but their party loyalty was greater than their commitment to women's suffrage. Liberal Party leaders opposed reform, in part because they believed the majority of women enfranchised would vote Conservative. While Conservative Party conferences repeatedly endorsed women's suffrage, and Conservative leaders expressed their support for it, they made no attempt to introduce legislation when in office, perhaps because the vast majority of Conservative MPs opposed it. This stalemate might have been overcome if public opinion had been aroused in support of reform but Becker and other leaders preferred secret negotiations with parliamentary cliques. By the 1880s Radical suffragists in the north of England were becoming frustrated with this strategy, and urged that mass suffrage demonstrations be organized to demonstrate public support for reform [61]

PARTY LOYALTY

The struggle over the 1884 women's suffrage amendment increased the tendency for suffragists to polarize along party lines. Radical suffragists were incensed at Becker's willingness to support legislation enfranchising only unmarried women. Becker's tactical alliance with the Conservative Party widened the breech between her and Liberal suffragists who advocated working through the Liberal Party. Some suffragists feared a permanent separation between reformers like Becker, who advocated allying with Conservatives for a restricted measure excluding married women, and those who insisted on working through the Liberal Party for a broader measure which would include them [61].

Suffragists were also disheartened by the emergence of organized female anti-suffragism in the late 1880s. Concerned that the Conservative government might grant suffrage to propertied spinsters and widows in the expectation they would vote Conservative, male opponents encouraged female anti-suffragists to speak out against reform. Mary Ward drafted an 'Appeal Against the Extension of the Parliamentary Franchise to Women' which was published in the *Nineteenth Century* in 1889 [*Doc. 4*]. Reform was opposed on the grounds that women's participation in politics was made impossible 'either by the disabilities of sex, or by strong formations of custom and habit resting ultimately upon physical difference . . . '. Beatrice Potter (later Webb), Mrs Leslie Stephen, and Mrs H. H. Asquith were among the 104 prominent women who signed the appeal [53]. Suffragists pointed out that many of those who signed were titled ladies whose class position ensured they suffered less from gender disabilities than women lower down the social hierarchy [*Doc. 5*].

Women were increasingly active in politics after the 1883 Corrupt Practices Act became law. By making it illegal to employ paid agents to do canvassing and other election work, the Act resulted in parties relying upon unpaid volunteers, chiefly women. Once their dependence on female volunteer workers became clear, political parties established female auxiliary organizations. The Women's Liberal Federation was formed in 1887 from several local women's associations; by 1896 it had 82,000 members. The Conservative Party's Primrose League allowed women to become members shortly after it was established in 1883, and by 1891 its female membership was estimated at 500,000 [114, 57].

Party work strengthened women's conviction that they should be enfranchised, but the parties preferred that the women's organizations subordinate women's suffrage to party objectives. Although the Conservative Party endorsed women's suffrage at its 1887 annual conference and reaffirmed support at later conferences, the Primrose League was not permitted to become a women's suffrage lobby. When the NSWS asked the league in 1886 what its position was on women's suffrage, the latter replied that the 'Executive Committee of the Ladies' Grand Council cannot enter into questions of contentious politics' [77 *p. 23*].

Liberal women had greater autonomy. Many had been active in the women's suffrage movement before helping to establish Women's Liberal Associations, and intended to use the Liberal Party's women's groups to pressure the party to support women's suffrage legislation. In 1892 Gladstone's opposition to women's suffrage forced Liberal women to decide whether their highest loyalty was to the party or to women's suffrage. When pro-suffrage women gained control of the WLF in 1892, over 7,000 members split away to form the Women's National Liberal Association. The suffragists who remained in the WLF continued to be torn between party and gender loyalty. At the 1896 WLF annual council those giving priority to the latter proposed that members should work only for Liberal candidates who supported women's suffrage. This motion was defeated; it was replaced by one which left local women's Liberal associations free to decide [101].

The women's party organizations growth contributed to the 1888 NSWS split. Because it was non-party the NSWS had not allowed women's party organizations to affiliate to it. But in 1888 when several local Women's Liberal Associations requested affiliation, a majority of NSWS members voted to change the rules. Following the vote Millicent Garrett Fawcett, Lydia Becker, and their followers withdrew from the NSWS and established a rival organization which retained the name 'Central Committee of the National Society for Women's Suffrage'. The majority of the societies adopted the new rules, and formed the Central National Society for Women's Suffrage.

Fawcett, who had recently withdrawn from the Liberal Party in protest against Gladstone's Irish Home Rule policy, viewed the rules change as an attempt by Liberal Party women to take over the NSWS. The new rules did result in the affiliation of Liberal women's groups to the NSWS, thereby strengthening the influence of Liberal women within it. In addition to this controversy, the nature of the society's demand was also an issue. The Central Committee continued to press for legislation which would have excluded married women. The Central National Society for Women's Suffrage was divided on the point; to avoid splitting its membership it supported bills that excluded married women as well as those which included them.

The conflict over whether married women should be included in the demand gave rise to a new suffrage society explicitly committed to that reform: the Women's Franchise League. Begun by Elizabeth Wolstenholme Elmy in 1889, it became the voice of ultra-Radical suffragism. While the older suffrage societies were willing to drop married women from their proposed suffrage legislation in order to increase its chances of being accepted, the League rejected this compromise strategy.

The League also made special efforts to link with working-class women and with the Labour movement. The League's leaders based their claim for women's suffrage on an economic view of citizenship which implied that capitalism was part of the problem. They held that women's labour, whether it be unpaid reproductive work or paid labour, entitled them to full citizenship rights. This provided a useful counter to the anti-suffrage argument that the vote should be limited to men because they could be called upon to risk their lives to defend the empire [61].

Although the suffrage campaign had been mainly a middle-class movement prior to 1890, working-class women's involvement grew significantly in the 1890s. In 1894 the Women's Co-operative Guild's annual conference endorsed women's suffrage, and nearly one-quarter of the Guildswomen signed the parliamentary petition that the national suffrage organization was circulating [101, 81]. Under the leadership of Esther Roper* and Eva Gore Booth from 1894, the North of England Society* (previously the Manchester Society) deliberately sought to draw working-class women into the suffrage movement. In order to refute the widely held view that only middle- and upper-class women desired the vote, Roper and Booth initiated a women's suffrage petition signed exclusively by working-class women. Within a year they had obtained 29,359 signatures and the petition was presented to the House of Commons [81].

LOCAL GOVERNMENT FRANCHISE

The 1894 Local Government Act is now viewed as an important turning-point in the suffrage campaign. It was significant in that it removed the issue of coverture from the franchise reform debate by making married women eligible to vote in all the local elections in which single women and widows could. This contributed to the expansion of female voting in local government elections in the 1890s; by 1900 women comprised 13.7 per cent of the local government electorate [101]. Also, by eliminating one of the important issues dividing reformers, it made possible the reunion of the leading suffrage organizations in 1897.

The reunion of the suffrage movement emerged out of the co-operation between the two national suffrage societies in securing some 257,000 signatures to a women's suffrage petition in the mid-1890s. Fawcett presided at the 1896 joint meeting of suffrage societies which agreed to form the National Union of Women's Suffrage Societies (NUWSS).* The new organization that came into being the following year was a federation of seventeen of the largest suffrage societies. Although its executive was expected to co-ordinate the member societies' activities, it had almost no power over them and no funds of its own. During its early years the NUWSS was primarily a liaison committee linking parliament and the member societies; it bore little resemblance to the powerful body it became later [62].

The new organization's rules reflected Fawcett's views. Its sole purpose was to secure votes for women, and the member societies were to be strictly neutral regarding political parties. This was a defeat for those who wanted the NUWSS to seek other gender reforms in addition to suffrage or who wanted formal ties with the Liberal Party. The Women's Franchise League, for example, did not join the NUWSS because its objectives were not limited to the vote. The

NUWSS's objective was to obtain the parliamentary suffrage for women on the same terms 'as it is, or may be granted to men' [62 p. 7].

Historians disagree on the state of the suffrage movement at the end of the nineteenth century. Female historians from both the constitutional and the militant movements concluded that it had come to a standstill. Strachey maintained that in 1900 the likelihood of reform seemed to be 'farther away than ever before in the history of the agitation' [28 p. 284] [Doc. 6]. Sylvia Pankhurst* described the movement as having 'sunk into an almost moribund coma of hopelessness' [22 p. 50]. This view is supported by Harrison's study of women's organizations' annual income, which indicates a sharp decline in financial support following the 1884 Reform Bill; it dropped to a low in the 1890s before reviving after 1900 [54].

Recently, however, some historians have begun to re-evaluate the late Victorian suffrage movement. David Rubenstein views the 1890s as a period of 'steady progress', and rejects the view that there was a sharp break between it and the following decade. He cites the growth of mass support as indicated by the 1896 petition (the largest parliamentary petition since the Chartist movement), the widening of the movement's social base through the increased involvement of working-class women and the origins of support for more militant methods as the failure of parliamentary lobbying became evident [101]. In *Suffrage Days* Sandra Holton develops this approach even further, finding the roots of militancy and democratic suffragism in new groups, such as the Women's Franchise League, which emerged in the 1890s [61]. Perhaps most important of all, as Philippa Levine suggests, was the creation of a sense of female solidarity through their 'celebration of their own moral superiority' over men [77 p. 19]. The development of this women's consciousness encouraged women to view themselves as a distinct sex-class, which overrode the fissureous tendencies of class and party differences.

2   THE NATIONAL UNION OF WOMEN'S SUFFRAGE SOCIETIES, 1897–1910

The women's suffrage movement has been portrayed as being nearly moribund during the early years of the twentieth century until the Women's Social and Political Union brought new life to it. This view assumes the WSPU was responsible for obtaining women's suffrage, and places the NUWSS in the background. This interpretation underestimates the NUWSS's importance. The NUWSS was a much stronger organization by 1910 than it had been in 1900, and this improvement began around 1902, before the WSPU was founded. NUWSS income and membership rose steadily after 1902, while the number of affiliated societies increased from 17 to 31 between 1902 and 1906 [54, 58].

Although it has been overshadowed by the more flamboyant WSPU, the NUWSS's transformation was one of the most significant developments in the suffrage movement between 1897 and 1910. At the beginning of the twentieth century the societies which belonged to the NUWSS were independent bodies that carried out most of the important suffrage work. The NUWSS co-ordinated their work and served as a liaison between them and parliament but had no funds of its own and little authority over them. The local societies appointed NUWSS Executive Committee members and viewed them as their representatives [62].

The NUWSS initiated a more aggressive stage in the suffrage campaign by convening a National Convention in Defence of the Civic Rights of Women in 1903. Aware that a general election was approaching, the delegates requested the NUWSS to form a committee immediately in every electoral district to press the question of women's suffrage on every parliamentary candidate before the next election and to attempt to persuade local party associations to select only candidates committed to women's suffrage. In order to implement this scheme the NUWSS began to exercise greater control over its member societies, and shifted its focus from parliament to the parliamentary constituencies. All of the candidates in the 1906 general election were questioned about their position on women's suffrage, and 415 pledged support for it [62].

The Women's Liberal Federation (WLF) also intervened in the election to increase support for suffrage by Liberal candidates. Liberal suffragists had long maintained that Liberal women were being used as 'Political Charwomen' – i.e., they did the electoral dirty work for candidates even though the party did not consider them suitable to be voters. At its 1902 annual council meeting the WLF adopted a resolution forbidding the WLF executive from lending assistance to anti-suffrage candidates. The WLF's national office ordinarily provided experienced female activists to conduct canvassing in the local constituencies; this was especially important during by-elections. Although local associations were exempt from the ban, the denial of trained operatives from the national office could substantially diminish the candidate's prospects. In thirteen of the twenty by-elections between May 1904 and November 1905 the Liberal candidate provided a written pledge to vote for women's suffrage; in five of the seven by-elections in which the candidate refused to pledge, assistance was denied [121].

THE NEW LIBERAL GOVERNMENT

There was a surge of optimism within the NUWSS about the prospects for reform when the 1906 Liberal government was formed with a huge majority in a parliament in which the majority of MPs were pledged to women's suffrage. Although officially non-partisan, the NUWSS considered women's suffrage a natural extension of liberal principles and had always assumed the Liberal Party would enfranchise women. Underlying this conviction was the mistaken belief that reform would emerge when a majority of backbenchers had been intellectually converted to the justice of the cause. Although a majority of Liberals supported women's suffrage, party and electoral considerations blocked reform: the issue divided the party so deeply that proceeding with reform risked a party split, and granting the NUWSS's demand for equal suffrage rights was expected to enfranchise women who would be mainly Conservative voters.

The NUWSS's confidence in the Liberal government was jolted almost immediately. The Prime Minister, Henry Campbell-Bannerman, met with a deputation from the NUWSS and other women's societies, but refused to make any pledge regarding suffrage and bluntly informed them that it was not realistic to expect the Liberal government to introduce legislation. At least one member of the deputation, Margaret Ashton, who spoke on behalf of the Women's Liberal Federations, was so disillusioned by Campbell-Bannerman's reply that she began working for Labour Party candidates. This was to become increasingly common in the following years [112].

THE MUD MARCH

WSPU militancy in 1906 generated considerable publicity which increased women's support for suffrage, and left the NUWSS seeking new ways to prove that it was equally vigorous in fighting for reform [*Doc. 7*]. It responded by organizing a series of open-air processions to demonstrate mass support for women's suffrage. The first of these, the 'Mud March' of February 1907, was the largest open-air demonstration ever held to that point. Although some 3,000 women representing 40 organizations participated, the WSPU did not because the Women's Liberal Federation refused to take part if the WSPU was invited [110]. The Mud March had a considerable impact because of the novelty of the spectacle, but even more so because of the impropriety of respectable women marching in the streets. Participating required a degree of courage beyond that needed for subsequent processions; the marchers risked their reputations, their employment, and ridicule from the crowds [110].

Prior to 1907 the decentralization of authority within the NUWSS hampered effective action; in that year it adopted a new constitution which substantially strengthened the NUWSS and its executive committee. Instead of being delegates representing the constituent societies which appointed them, the new constitution encouraged executive committee members to view issues from the NUWSS's perspective by providing that they be elected for a one year term, thus giving them greater permanence. Under the new constitution the executive committee was responsible to a council of representatives from the local societies that met quarterly to set policies. Following the adoption of the new constitution, the NUWSS for the first time moved into its own offices, hired full-time staff and controlled its own funds [62]. Although the reorganization was intended to make the NUWSS a more effective fighting force, its democratic constitution also drew attention to the contrast between its governing structure and that of the WSPU.

The new constitution also strengthened Millicent Fawcett's authority to speak for the NUWSS by providing for an elected president. Fawcett did not assume this position uncontested. Delegates at the 1907 council meeting elected her over Lady Francis Balfour, President of the London Society for Women's Suffrage (LSWS) and sister-in-law of Arthur Balfour, the Conservative Party leader [102].

If the NUWSS's faith in the Liberal Party as a vehicle of reform during this period seems excessive, it is mistaken to attribute this to Fawcett's personal loyalty to that party. She left the Liberal Party in protest against Gladstone's Irish Home Rule Bill and never returned. Fawcett became a Liberal Unionist, but in 1904 resigned from the Women's Liberal Unionist Association when it supported the Conservative Party's policy of protection. Although her commitment to free trade prevented her from belonging to the Conservative and Unionist Party, her biographer defines her political position as 'Unionist-leaning' [102 *p. 183*]. As late as 1910 she publicly attacked key Liberal government policies, and remained resolutely hostile to Irish Home Rule even though it was a central part of the Liberal Government's legislative programme after 1910.

The importance of Conservative women in the NUWSS, and in the suffrage movement in general, has been underestimated. Fawcett considered Lady Balfour to be her first lieutenant; Balfour was one of the NUWSS's founders and had been a dominant figure in the LSWS for many years [100]. Lady Selborne, the daughter of former Prime Minister Lord Salisbury, and Arthur Balfour's cousin, became President of the Conservative and Unionist Women's Franchise Association (CUWFA)* when it was formed in 1907. The CUWFA lobbied the Conservative Party for women's suffrage. Although they considered encouraging Conservative women to refuse to do election work for anti-suffrage Conservative candidates, they concentrated on convincing Conservatives that granting the vote to women who met existing property qualifications had important electoral advantages for the party. The CUWFA claimed that in addition to enfranchising women who would mainly be Conservative voters, a limited measure of women's suffrage was the best means of heading off the movement for adult male suffrage [87]. By 1913 the CUWFA had 53 branches, more than its better publicized Liberal counterpart [129].

INTERNAL TENSIONS

The NUWSS included suffragists from across the political spectrum, and unsurprisingly there were sharp clashes reflecting divergent class and political outlook. The split between democratic suffragists, mainly from the northern societies, and conservative suffragists, who dominated the LSWS, was a growing source of tension within the NUWSS after 1907. The increased power granted the NUWSS executive over policy making by the 1907 constitution came at the expense of the provincial societies, and they were dissatisfied with the continued control of the executive by conservative women, many of whom were LSWS members. The struggle culminated at the 1910 council meeting with the adoption of a more decentralized structure involving the formation of regional federations over the objections of the executive and the LSWS [112].

Historians traditionally have portrayed the NUWSS and the WSPU as rivals, and stressed the differences between them. Sandra Holton, however, suggests that, at least until 1909, they be viewed as two wings of the same movement in a 'symbiotic' relationship [58]. Jo Vellacott agrees, although she views the break between the two organizations as occurring around 1908 when the WSPU shifted to window-breaking in addition to disrupting Liberal meetings [112]. Both agree that tensions between the groups increased substantially after 1909; by 1914 Fawcett considered the WSPU militants to be the 'chief obstacles' to achieving suffrage [102 *p. 177*].

Although some NUWSS members had reservations about the WSPU, until 1908 these were overshadowed by recognition that it was strengthening the suffrage movement. NUWSS members were often sympathetic towards the early forms of militancy which involved civil disobedience with no harm to property or other persons. In 1906, Fawcett admitted that in the past twelve months militancy had done more to make suffrage 'practical politics' than constitutional methods had in the past twelve years, and acknowledged that the WSPU's activities had contributed significantly to the NUWSS's membership growth after 1905 [102]. Until 1908 many WSPU members also belonged to the NUWSS and both organizations accepted this without any sense of inconsistency [62, 58].

The NUWSS support for militancy was strongest when it involved WSPU women becoming martyrs for the suffrage cause by undergoing arrest and imprisonment. But NUWSS opinion swung against the WSPU when it changed in 1908 to attacks on property and people. Reluctant to criticize the WSPU publicly, Fawcett privately thought the WSPU's encouraging working-class 'toughs' and unemployed workers to join them in using 'brute force' to rush the House of Commons in 1908 was the act of a 'dastard' or a woman gone 'mad' [62] [*Doc. 8*]. In November 1908 the NUWSS made the breach public by sending a letter to MPs and the press expressing its 'strong objection' to the use of violence, and officially dissociating itself from the WSPU [102, 62]. When the WSPU invited the NUWSS to join them in a united demonstration late in 1909, the NUWSS declined,

ating that there were 'questions of principle at stake' which made it essential that the constitutional suffragists 'separate themselves completely from those who employ different methods' [110, *p. 111*].

The conflict between the NUWSS and the WSPU was focused on the merits of militant methods, but it also raised ideological differences. Fawcett's belief that women's nature was different and morally superior to men's underlay her objection to the WSPU's resort to force [*Doc. 9*]. Given her conviction that the women's suffrage movement was an appeal against government by physical force, it is not surprising that she viewed the WSPU's use of force as undermining the movement's moral foundation. By resorting to force and behaving like men, the WSPU not only undermined the ideology of sexual difference, it also undermined the notion of female moral superiority thus, in Fawcett's view, weakening women's claim for the franchise [60].

Although Fawcett's efforts to prevent conflict between the NUWSS and the WSPU had enabled suffrage advocates to belong to both organizations, by 1908 the NUWSS had become so alarmed by the WSPU's tactics that it officially committed its members to using only 'constitutional' methods in working for reform. This placed pressure on WSPU members who also belonged to NUWSS local societies to choose between the two; open conflict broke out in some societies. Constitutionalists and WSPU supporters struggled for control of the London Society for Women's Suffrage in 1908 following the NUWSS's public condemnation of militant methods. At the 1908 LSWS annual meeting four WSPU members who also belonged to the LSWS formally proposed that the LSWS adopt the WSPU's anti-Liberal by-election policy, and that LSWS executive committee members not be allowed to hold office in party organizations, a move intended to exclude Liberal women from the LSWS executive [62].

The NUWSS and LSWS executives viewed this as a WSPU attempt to seize control of the LSWS, and in a tense struggle succeeded in defeating both resolutions. Fawcett spoke against the resolutions, urging LSWS members to resign if they could not accept the NUWSS policy of opposition to unlawful methods. During the following three months 133 LSWS members did resign, but this was offset by the addition of 293 new members [58].

The clash with the WSPU also led the NUWSS to begin publishing its own journal. Previously the NUWSS contributed to *The Women's Franchise*, an independent suffrage journal which printed reports from the WSPU and the WFL in addition to the NUWSS. Concerned that this would encourage the public to link the NUWSS with the militant groups, the NUWSS established *The Common Cause* in 1909

ially by Helena Swanwick, by 1912 *The Common*
ation of 10,000 [102].
for the NUWSS's journal drew attention to a dis-
the NUWSS and the WSPU which grew in
importance after 1910. While the latter viewed itself as a women's
movement promoting gender solidarity, the NUWSS accepted male
members, rejected 'setting the women against men', and considered
itself to be working for the 'common cause of humanity' [58 *p. 66*].
Fawcett recognized that allowing anti-suffragists to portray the suffrage campaign as part of a sex-war waged by women would only
hamper efforts to persuade an all-male parliament to pass suffrage
legislation, but she also sincerely believed that a sex-war was impossible [*Doc. 10*].

In other respects, however, it is the ideological similarity between
the NUWSS and the WSPU which seems most apparent. Both drew
upon a heightened gender consciousness which encouraged an un-
usual degree of gender unity between women of different classes.
Although the WSPU's concern with women's sexual exploitation is
better known, recent research has drawn attention to its importance
in Fawcett's ideology [38]. Some NUWSS members, such as Lady
Chance, viewed the women's movement as a great moral movement,
and claimed that the demand for suffrage was rooted in the belief
that women would not be able to eradicate the evils arising from
male sexual exploitation of women until they had the vote [73]
[*Doc. 11*].

Anti-suffragists used the women's rhetoric of gender unity to encourage men to believe that masculinity was under attack and to urge
that men bond together to resist this subversive movement. The suffrage campaign's gender dimensions thus created special problems for
its male supporters [69]. Anti-suffragists impugned their masculinity
and denounced them as 'traitors to the masculine cause' [107]. Despite this, male suffrage organizations sprang up in various parts of
Britain: the Men's League for Women's Suffrage (established 1907)
was based in London; Scottish men formed the Northern Men's
Federation for Women's Suffrage in 1913 [125]; and the Manchester
Men's League for Women's Suffrage was created in 1908 [128]. The
existence of the men's organizations undermined the anti-suffragist
claim that the suffrage struggle was part of a sex-war in which masculinity implied opposition to women's suffrage.

Early in 1908 a Liberal MP, Henry Stanger, introduced a private
member's bill on women's suffrage. The NUWSS felt very encouraged
when it passed its second reading with a 179 vote majority even

though it was not granted parliamentary time to proceed fui
This was the first occasion since 1897 that parliament had taken fa
ourable action on a women's suffrage bill, and the bill's substantial
Liberal support strengthened the NUWSS conviction that the Liberal
Party would enact reform [62].

This strategy became questionable when Herbert Henry Asquith, a
determined anti-suffragist, became prime minister later in 1908.
Shortly after he assumed office, a deputation of 60 Liberal MPs met
with him to request that additional parliamentary time be provided
for the Stanger bill. Although he admitted that about two-thirds of
the cabinet and a majority of the Liberal Party favoured reform,
Asquith refused. Instead, he proposed that the government sponsor a
manhood-suffrage bill which could be amended to include women's
suffrage, and pledged that he would not oppose such an amendment
if it were 'democratic'. NUWSS leaders viewed this as a ruse to pla-
cate the women's suffrage advocates while avoiding reform. Asquith
knew very well that many of the MPs who supported equal franchise
rights would not support a measure extending it to all women. While
appearing to grant a concession, Asquith was actually ensuring its defeat by insisting that the amendment be 'democratic'. This
interpretation was confirmed a few days later when Asquith acknowledged in parliament that he did not expect women's suffrage to
emerge in the foreseeable future [87].

DEMOCRATIC SUFFRAGISTS

Asquith's expression of support for an adult suffrage measure heightened the tensions between reformers urging that women be
enfranchised as part of an adult suffrage measure and those, like
Fawcett, who advocated the franchise for women on the same terms
that men had it. In 1908 encouraged by Asquith's pledge, women
trade unionists joined with the Women's Co-operative Guild (WCG)
to establish the People's Suffrage Federation (PSF)* to work for adult
suffrage. Led by Margaret Llewelyn Davies, the WCG general secretary, the PSF believed that working-class women should be included
in suffrage reform and that this could best be achieved by linking
women's suffrage to the movement for a democratic franchise. Davies
coined the term 'democratic suffragists' to refer to those who took
this approach [58].

Davies and her supporters saw several advantages to pressing for
adult suffrage. They believed that class divisions were undermining
suffragist efforts to create a sense of gender solidarity. Democratic

suffragists objected to equal franchise because it would reinforce the class structure by granting the vote to elite propertied women. Adult suffrage, however, would avoid this by enfranchising working-class women. It also had greater partisan appeal to Liberals than equal suffrage. Many Liberals feared that the NUWSS demand for suffrage on the same basis that men had it would enfranchise women likely to vote Conservative, whereas adult suffrage would increase the number of Liberal voters [112].

Both WSPU and NUWSS leaders opposed adult suffrage. Fawcett did not think there was any great pressure in the country for adult suffrage and was convinced the change would make reform much more difficult to achieve. But there was significant support for adult suffrage within the NUWSS; its secretary, Marion Phillips, had been one of the PSF founders. Convinced that adult suffrage was a trap, Fawcett prevented democratic suffragists from changing NUWSS policy; Phillips resigned as NUWSS secretary in 1910, apparently as a result of the conflict [102, 58].

ANTI-SUFFRAGIST ORGANIZED OPPOSITION

Anti-suffragists were so alarmed by the improved prospects for reform in 1908 that they began to organize. A parliamentary committee of male anti-suffragists urged female opponents to set up an organization to resist reform. In July 1908 the Women's National Anti-Suffrage League (WNAL)* was established with Lady Jersey chairing the executive committee, but with Mrs. Humphrey Ward as the real driving force within the organization. Later that year it merged with the men's anti-suffrage league to form the National League for Opposing Women's Suffrage. By 1914 it had 42,000 members, many of them wealthy and influential. Lord Rothschild was the Anti-Suffrage League's leading financial supporter, while the others included some of Britain's most prominent bankers, brewers and coal and steel magnates [53, 87].

Female anti-suffragists presented a variety of arguments against women voting in parliamentary elections. Most of these were based on assumptions about sexual difference linked to the idea of separate spheres. Violet Markham, prominent in the WNAL, insisted that women's nature had a distinct spiritual quality that men's lacked. She feared that women would lose their special qualities and sink to the men's level if they entered political life on equal terms with men. While she urged women to participate in local government because it involved areas such as education which were a part of the women's sphere, she did not think women were suited to vote in parliamentary elections because these were concerned with the defence of the empire which was beyond women's experience. While her objection rested in part on the notion that women would not be knowledgeable about an area outside their sphere, it also stemmed from a conviction that matters involving physical force were part of the male sphere. Many female anti-suffragists, including Markham, feared participation in decisions to use physical force would corrupt women's spiritual nature and erode the differences between women and men [16].

Some earlier accounts portrayed the NUWSS as a group of self-interested middle-class women narrowly concerned with the vote to enhance their status. This is misleading in several respects. The NUWSS believed that the vote would transform women's place in society and gender relationships. It maintained that women would gain economic independence, increased job opportunities, higher wages and improved marriages from the vote [47]. It was the NUWSS member, Ada Nield Chew, who attacked 'the ideal of the domestic tabby cat woman as that to which all womanhood should aspire' [47 p. 20]. Chew considered the assumption that all women are especially suited for domestic tasks to be as absurd as claiming all men are suited to be engineers [20].

Historians have only recently begun to explore the implications of national identity for the women's suffrage movement. Although the NUWSS and the WSPU portrayed themselves as British women's movements, both were led by English women who tended to view the struggle from an English perspective. While welcoming the emergence of a British women's movement, Irish, Welsh, and Scottish women were alert to the danger that it might become an instrument of English cultural hegemony.

Welsh suffragists tended to join the NUWSS rather than the WSPU. While the WSPU imported English 'stars' to address its Welsh meetings, the NUWSS relied on Welsh women in building a democratic organization [41]. By 1913 the Cardiff and District Women's Suffrage Society was the largest NUWSS society outside London [41]. The NUWSS recognized the Welsh Home Rule movement could benefit the suffrage campaign; NUWSS lobbying helped ensure that the 1914 Welsh Home Rule Bill granted women the right to vote for the proposed Welsh regional parliament [112]. Welsh suffragists signalled their Welsh identity in a variety of ways: they established the Cymric Suffrage Union, translated suffrage pamphlets into Welsh and participated in the 1911 London suffrage procession dressed in a (spurious) Welsh folk costume [41, 110].

Scottish women, campaigning under the slogan, 'ye mauna tramp on the Scottish thistle', developed a suffrage movement with a distinct Scottish identity. Insisting on a greater degree of independence than the Welsh women's movement, they formed separate federations with some degree of autonomy within each of the national suffrage organizations. By 1914 the NUWSS's Scottish Federation had 63 societies with 7,370 members. Although they shared a sense of gender unity with English women, Scottish women recognized that the suffrage movement could be used to impose an English cultural identity on them. They protested when the NUWSS referred to its 1911 suffrage procession (which included Scottish women) as the 'March of England's Women' [35]. On at least one occasion the Scottish women brought about the dismissal of the English organizer the NUWSS sent to Scotland on the ground that she was incompatible with the Scots. They also resisted the efforts by the NUWSS's Election Fighting Fund committee to control the EFF work in Scotland [75].

Further research on the relationship between religion and the suffrage movement is needed. Although church membership is often assumed to have made women less likely to participate in female reform movements such as the suffrage campaign, it is clear that religion strengthened some women's commitment to reform.

Catholic feminists established the Catholic Women's Suffrage Society (CWSS) early in 1911 to encourage more Catholic women to join the suffrage campaign. Although some individual members were active in the WSPU or the WFL, the CWSS became a constitutional society with branches in Liverpool and Wimbledon; by 1913 it claimed 1,000 members. It participated in the London coronation procession in 1911 and signed the Jewish League's resolution against forced feeding of suffrage prisoners; its leaders supported the Tax Resistance League until the CWSS rank-and-file objected [126].

Participation in the suffrage campaign by Church of England women grew out of a prior campaign for the right of women to have the vote in church councils. Many of them joined the Church League for Women's Suffrage, formed in 1909, which was led by the Reverend Claude Hinscliff and Maude Royden [44]. A constitutional society, it had over 5,000 members by April 1914. Some of its members established the Suffragist Churchwomen's Protest Committee; in 1914 Alice Kidd, its secretary, informed the Archbishop of Canterbury that the committee objected to the 'servile attitude of the Heads of the Church towards an unjust and irresponsible government' [55 p. 106].

With a general election approaching, Liberal women were torn between gender and party loyalty. Asquith's opposition to women's suffrage resulted in demands that Liberal women should refuse to do election work for Liberal candidates who were not proven friends of reform and there was pressure within the NUWSS to adopt an anti-Liberal election policy. The issue became a matter of heated controversy in 1909 when Caroline Osler, President of an NUWSS affiliate, the Birmingham Suffrage Society, appeared on the platform with Asquith at a Liberal Party rally shortly after a suffragist meeting to protest against the exclusion of women from Asquith's meetings. Attacked publicly for placing party loyalty ahead of the suffrage cause, Osler resigned from her position in the local WLF shortly afterwards. Three other officers in the local WLF followed her example, and *The Common Cause* carried reports of other women's resignations from their WLF positions around this time. In 1910 the NUWSS rules were changed to require officers and executive committee members to pledge that they would 'put the interests of suffrage before party considerations' [58 p. 50].

The announcement of the January 1910 general election brought renewed optimism about the prospects for reform. Responding to pressure from the Women's Liberal Federation, Asquith pledged at the beginning of the election campaign that the Liberal government, if returned to office, would allow a free vote in the House of Commons on a women's suffrage amendment to a Reform bill. Winston Churchill and Edward Grey also made encouraging statements about women's suffrage, leaving the impression that reform was likely if a majority of MPs supported it. In addition to pressuring candidates to include women's suffrage in their election addresses, the NUWSS organized voters' petitions at polling places to demonstrate that male voters also supported women's suffrage. In some places hostile police warned the suffragists that if they asked voters for signatures to the petition, they might be arrested for solicitation under the law intended to deal with prostitutes. Despite impediments such as this, almost 300,000 signatures were obtained and the NUWSS viewed it as a useful demonstration of male electoral support for the cause [112]. Although 323 members of the new House of Commons were pledged to some version of reform, the Liberal Party lost its majority and in the following years depended upon support from the Labour Party and the Irish Nationalists to remain in office [62].

The Liberal government's precarious position created an opportunity for suffragists to exert even greater pressure when a second general election became necessary in December 1910. Although the Women's Liberal Federation's executive committee refused to endorse any action that might jeopardize a Liberal victory, the acrimony generated by the debate at the 1910 WLF annual meeting demonstrated that some Liberal women activists were no longer willing to work for the re-election of a Liberal government which was not firmly committed to reform [121]. This alarmed Liberal MPs who realized that active support by Liberal women party workers was vital to their election prospects. One Liberal MP, Walter MacLaren, warned the Liberal Chief Whip, the Master of Elibank, that the party could not afford to alienate Liberal women party workers, and therefore should pledge that it would provide facilities for a women's suffrage bill in the next parliament [87]. About two weeks later Asquith made such a pledge, thus permitting the NUWSS and Liberal women to work for Liberal candidates considered friends of reform.

The suffrage campaign made substantial progress during the first decade of the twentieth century. The NUWSS began its transformation from an organization dominated by middle-class London women to a national movement with a much broader social base among women from a variety of ethnic, religious and class backgrounds. Whereas prior to 1900 suffragists were still seeking to persuade MPs of the merits of the issue, by 1910 a majority had been converted to the cause [90]. What remained was to determine what form of reform would be acceptable to parliament, and to find a means of forcing the government either to sponsor legislation or at least not to impede passage of a bill favoured by a parliamentary majority.

3 THE WOMEN'S SOCIAL AND POLITICAL UNION, 1903–1914

The WSPU's role in enfranchising women is controversial. Although non-historians often assume it was chiefly, if not solely, responsible for obtaining women's suffrage, historians are much more sceptical about its contribution. It is generally agreed that at first the WSPU revitalized the suffrage campaign, but that after 1910 its escalation of militancy impeded reform. Recent writing about the WSPU has shifted from claiming that it was responsible for women's suffrage to stressing its contribution to feminist culture [113].

The WSPU began in the north of England, but a vigorous women's suffrage movement already existed in that region when it was established. Led by Esther Roper and Eva Gore-Booth, the North of England Society for Women's Suffrage (NESWS) concentrated on securing working-class women's support by working with local labour and trade-union organizations. Roper and Gore-Booth drew Christabel Pankhurst* into the NESWS in 1901, and Christabel later acknowledged that she had served her political apprenticeship in the suffrage movement under them [21]. But by 1903 Christabel had begun to rebel against their leadership. She considered Labour's support for women's suffrage to be half-hearted, and she had little enthusiasm for the drudgery involved in building a mass organization by grass-roots political work [81]. When she learned her mother was proposing to form a new women's suffrage organization, Christabel welcomed the opportunity to change her affiliation.

Emmeline Pankhurst* established the Women's Social and Political Union* in Manchester in October 1903. Active in the Independent Labour Party (and elected to its National Administrative Council in 1904), she attempted to persuade it to support votes for women on the same terms that men had it. Sceptical of the men's commitment, Mrs Pankhurst formed a women-only group which was originally intended to pressure the ILP to make a firm commitment to reform. She invited a number of working-class women, most of them wives of ILP members, to her Manchester home to establish the new organization which took as its motto: 'Deeds, not words' [99 *p. 30*].

MILITANCY AND THE WSPU

Although the WSPU was not at first a militant organization, 'deeds' soon came to mean militant methods. Several WSPU members had become familiar with militant methods while active in the Women's Franchise League in the 1890s: Mrs Pankhurst, Dora Montefiore and Elizabeth Wolstenholme Elmy among others. Montefiore was one of the London WSPU's founders and from the beginning urged civil disobedience in the form of tax-resistance [61]. In 1906 after having refused to pay taxes because 'taxation without representation is tyranny', Montefiore's house was beseiged for six weeks by bailiffs seeking to seize her property [61 *p. 112*].

Christabel claimed militancy began in 1905 when she interrupted a Liberal political rally in Manchester with a demand that it endorse votes for women [21]. During the disturbance she deliberately committed a technical assault on a policeman in order to be arrested. She correctly anticipated this would generate publicity which would revive the suffrage issue, and attract new members to the WSPU. Her actions shocked contemporaries. The contrast with the NUWSS members' polite, lady-like behaviour was obvious and intentional. Instead of sitting quietly while men did the talking, as was customary in public meetings, Christabel deliberately sought to undermine gender boundaries. This was one reason many young middle-class women prefered the WSPU to the NUWSS.

Militancy was a rebellion against Edwardian gender roles and their restrictions on women's personal freedom [*Doc. 12*]. Part of the WSPU's appeal stemmed from the perception that it was fighting for independence for women, not just for the vote [113, 60]. Militancy gave women the opportunity to repudiate what Christabel called the 'slave spirit' [*Doc. 13*]. This is why Christabel insisted she didn't want the vote to be given to women; they would be empowered only if they forced the government to concede it [102].

Christabel's introduction of militant methods contributed to her rupture with Roper and the NESWS. Roper originally thought it was a courageous act but she later considered it to be a publicity stunt that would discredit other suffragists [81]. She was also disillusioned by Christabel's dishonesty in portraying herself as an innocent victim when she had deliberately sought arrest [*Doc. 14*]. Northern working-class women feared that Christabel's behaviour would undermine the work they had done to recruit women to the suffrage movement. Roper complained that working-class women were being held accountable for the biting and spitting by women of higher social standing. Because of this, working-class women were reluctant to take part in public demonstrations, thus undermining the radical suffragist attempt to build a mass-based movement [81].

Engaging in acts of militancy required considerable courage, as they aroused intense male hostility that frequently led to violence at public meetings. Suffragettes who interrupted political meetings were frequently pummelled by men in the audience and handled roughly by stewards. In some instances, especially outside London, suffragette meetings were disrupted by bands of young males, often with the police refusing to intervene [*Doc. 15*].

WSPU militancy encouraged the perception that it had a more radical objective than the NUWSS. This is misleading: during most of the prewar period both the WSPU and the NUWSS sought votes for women on an equal basis with men. Equal franchise meant most working-class women would be excluded from voting. This did not disturb Christabel, who maintained that 'our [WSPU] main concern was not with the *numbers* of women to be enfranchised but with the removal of a stigma upon womanhood as such' [21 *p. 186*]. But Labour women objected that the WSPU's slogan 'Votes for Women' was deceptive. Working-class women attending WSPU meetings assumed it stood for votes for all women; they were dismayed to discover that working-class women would still be voteless even if the WSPU's demand was obtained. This is one reason why Sandra Holton claims the true divide within the suffrage movement was not between the WSPU and the NUWSS, but between the groups seeking equal franchise and those, such as the People's Suffrage Federation, which advocated adult suffrage [58].

WSPU militancy evolved through at least three distinct stages. Originally it involved interrupting Liberal speakers. In this stage, militancy was intended to generate public support for reform and involved acts of civil disobedience in which the militants endangered only themselves so that they could be seen as martyrs. In 1908 the purpose and the form of militancy changed. Convinced that public goodwill and broad popular support would not bring about legislation, the WSPU made limited threats to public order in an attempt to coerce the government into sponsoring suffrage legislation. This stage involved destruction of property, such as window breaking, and occasionally violence against members of the government [134]. The third stage emerged in 1913 and relied on the use of arson in secret attacks on private as well as public property in which the perpetrators attempted to avoid arrest [61, 69].

THE WSPU SPLITS FROM THE ILP

Although the WSPU had emerged from the ILP, by 1906 Christabel was determined to sever its link with the Labour movement. This enabled the WSPU to present itself as a women's movement independent of men's organizations. It also enhanced the WSPU's ability to recruit women from the social elite, many of them Conservatives, who would not have joined a working-class organization which supported the ILP. Convinced that the House of Commons was 'more impressed by the demonstrations of the feminine bourgeoisie than of the feminine proletariat', Christabel proceeded to alter the WSPU's class and party connections [21 *pp.* 66–7].

The WSPU's new policy shocked many ILP members when it was implemented during the 1906 Cockermouth by-election. During the campaign the WSPU contingent refused to endorse Robert Smellie, the Labour candidate who advocated adult suffrage, and concentrated on persuading the electorate to defeat the Liberal candidate. Although ostensibly a nonparty position, it encouraged votes for the Conservative candidate (the eventual winner) since he was the main alternative to the Liberal. At the Huddersfield by-election a few months later the WSPU refused again to support the Labour candidate even though he advocated women's suffrage [80]. Christabel's new policy forced ILP women to choose between the WSPU and the ILP; this was a major factor in the split within the ILP in 1907. In 1907, attacked by the ILP for having betrayed the movement, Christabel and Mrs Pankhurst formally resigned from the ILP.

The WSPU's separation from the political left and from its working-class roots was facilitated by moving its headquarters from Manchester to London in 1906. Given the Pankhursts' lack of money, the move became possible when Emmeline Pethick-Lawrence joined the WSPU and she and her husband, Frederick, offered their house at Clements Inn to the WSPU for its use. In addition to providing Christabel with an office, they allowed her to live in their house and treated her like a daughter. Emmeline became the WSPU's treasurer and with Fred's assistance dramatically improved its financial position. With Mrs Pankhurst and Christabel, she became part of the triumvirate which directed the WSPU until she and Fred were expelled in 1912.

The move to London led to tensions with Dora Montefiore who, with Sylvia, had been largely responsible for developing the London WSPU organization. A socialist who became a member of the Social Democratic Federation's executive in 1904, Dora used open-air meetings and concentrated on recruiting working-class women, both innovations within the London suffrage campaign. Dora established the WSPU's first London branch at Canning Town in 1906, but when she attempted to form additional branches without the Pankhursts' prior approval, they decided she was becoming too independent. In the ensuing conflict Dora withdrew from the WSPU. Her reasons for resigning included the Pankhursts' anti-Labour policy as well as their autocratic leadership [63, 86].

By 1907 Mrs Pankhurst was convinced that a Conservative government was most likely to introduce women's suffrage in an attempt to 'dish' the Liberals as they had in the 1867 Reform Act. Given her 'incipient Toryism', it is likely that Christabel encouraged this perception [22 *p. 221*]. In 1907 Christabel initiated a private correspondence with Arthur Balfour, the Conservative Party leader, seeking a firm pledge that the next Conservative government would sponsor women's suffrage legislation [99]. Although Balfour refused, the WSPU had so thoroughly alienated the Liberal and Labour Parties that it had no option but to continue hoping that the Conservative Party would endorse reform; by 1914 the WSPU was openly calling for the formation of a Conservative government [47].

Certainly this change reflected the political preferences of the upper-class women who comprised Christabel and Mrs Pankhurst's social network after they moved to London. Working-class women began to feel uncomfortable in what was becoming an elite women's organization. When Alice Milne came down from Manchester to visit the London WSPU headquarters in October 1906 she found it 'full of fashionable ladies in silks and satins' in sharp contrast to the Manchester office [81 *p. 206*]. Some working-class women began referring to the WSPU as 'the Society Women's Political Union' [58 *p. 37*].

The WSPU grew so rapidly following its move to London that by 1910 its income and paid staff exceeded that of the Labour Party. WSPU income increased from £2,900 in the year 1906–7 to £33,000 in 1909–10 [99], and the number of paid organizers increased from one to 30. Its journal, *Votes For Women*, begun in 1907, reached its peak circulation of almost 40,000 copies in 1909–10 [22]. Despite its northern origins, most of this growth was concentrated in London and the Home Counties. Although married women comprised a majority of WSPU members in the early years, it increasingly became a movement of young single women; the proportion of WSPU financial subscribers who were unmarried rose from 45 to 67 per cent between 1906–7 and 1910–11 [99].

In 1907 the WSPU's rapid growth contributed to its greatest internal crisis. Teresa Billington Greig's work as WSPU organizer resulted in an unusually rapid increase in the number of branches that year. Most of the new branches were in Scotland or the north of England. They had considerable autonomy; those in Scotland even established a Scottish Council with its own treasury [99]. ILP women were so prominent in the Scottish branches that they were sometimes mistaken for an ILP organization. They resisted the Pankhursts' orders not to support Labour candidates, and partly because of this, welcomed Billington Greig's effort to reduce the Pankhursts' domination of the WSPU.

THE FORMATION OF THE WOMEN'S FREEDOM LEAGUE

WSPU members who were Labour Party or ILP supporters resisted the WSPU split from the Labour movement. Eager to work for both suffrage and the Labour movement, Teresa Billington Greig drafted a constitution for consideration by the 1907 WSPU annual conference which would have established a democratic organization. Mrs Pankhurst responded by cancelling the annual meeting, rejecting the constitution and insisting the WSPU needed military discipline, not democracy. WSPU Executive Committee members Billington Greig, Charlotte Despard*, and Edith How-Martyn responded by forming the Women's Freedom League (WFL) in November 1907. About one-fifth of the WSPU members followed them, including many working-class women, such as Hannah Mitchell, who did not wish to break with the Labour Party. The withdrawal of many of the most active socialist women from the WSPU left it even more dependent on upper-class women with close ties to the Conservative Party [58].

With Despard as President, the WFL also became a militant society. In 1908 there were 142 separate imprisonments of WFL members [47]. In the following year, WFL members established the Women's Tax Resistance League which urged women to refuse to pay national taxes until they were granted the vote [88]. It also considered urging working-class women to limit the size of their families until suffrage was granted, but the WFL annual conference rejected the proposal following objections that it would encourage sexual immorality. Although the WFL had 53 branches, its membership was smaller than the WSPU's; in 1914 it claimed to have 4,000 members [47].

WSPU LEADERSHIP

Authority within the WSPU became even more centralized following the split. Although Mrs Pankhurst remained the WSPU's official leader, she had little interest in its daily administration and WSPU policy was thus usually set by Christabel and the Pethick-Lawrences. Annual conferences were no longer held, and its leaders increasingly referred to the WSPU as a military organization. Even WSPU activists were critical of this trend towards autocracy; indeed it was a factor in Dora Marsden's resignation in 1911 [46].

By 1908, although the WSPU had become openly autocratic the Pankhursts found it difficult to maintain control over their activists. Christabel's insistence that the WSPU was like an army reflected a desire for an authoritarian structure which was not achieved in practice [105]. This is evident in the introduction of new militant tactics by WSPU members without either Christabel's or Mrs Pankhurst's prior approval. This occurred in June 1908 when Mary Leigh and Edith New threw rocks through two windows of the prime minister's residence at 10 Downing Street in retaliation for the brutal treatment of suffragettes in Parliament Square by police and gangs of young men [99]. In response to the forced feeding of suffragettes, Marion Wallace Dunlop undertook the first hunger strike in July 1909 without the Pankhursts' prior knowledge [61]. WSPU members later spontaneously initiated more serious attacks on property which the Pankhursts endorsed afterwards [58].

Despite the Pankhursts' desire to have a tightly disciplined army, in practice they struggled to retain control over the more free spirited WSPU activists. The Lancashire militants associated with Mary Gaw-thorpe were especially difficult to control [61]. Although the WSPU portrayed Emily Davison as a martyr following her death, she and Mary Leigh were considered rebels by the Pankhursts because they could not control them. While some of the more independent activists resigned from the WSPU, others, such as Elinor Penn Gaskell and Rose Lamartine Yates, became open critics of the Pankhursts from within the union [105].

The 1908 Hyde Park mass meeting and the government's response marked an important turning-point in the WSPU's campaign. Shortly before he became prime minister, Asquith stated that he would abandon his opposition to women's suffrage if it was demonstrated that the majority of women desired the vote and that they and the community would benefit by having it. Christabel responded by planning the first mass suffrage demonstration. On 21 June 1908 seven processions wearing the WSPU colours – purple, white, and green – marched through the streets of London to Hyde Park, where they formed the largest mass meeting ever held, a crowd estimated at over 250,000 persons. When Asquith remained unmoved by this display of public support, the Pankhursts concluded that peaceful agitation was useless. They revived militancy, and in even more violent forms [99].

During most of 1910 the WSPU suspended militancy while the Conciliation Committee gathered support for its Conciliation Bill. Although the bill passed its second reading, it was shelved when the government declined to allow further parliamentary time for it in that session. When Asquith indicated no facilities would be provided for further consideration of the bill in the new parliamentary session, the WSPU sent a deputation of some 300 women to the House of Commons on 18 November.

BLACK FRIDAY

The clash with police that resulted has become known as 'Black Friday'. In the past when WSPU women attempted to rush past the police lines, they had been quickly and politely arrested. But on this occasion, instead of promptly arresting them, the police assaulted the women during a six-hour struggle. It appeared to witnesses as well as the victims that the police had deliberately attempted to subject the women to sexual humiliation in a public setting to teach them a lesson [*Doc. 16*]. When a female demonstrator objected to a policeman grabbing her by the hip, he replied: 'Oh, my old dear, I can grip you wherever I like today' [*99 p. 140*]. Some of the spectators joined in; others cheered the police on. Several of the women involved vowed that in the future they would engage in some actionable offense, such as window-breaking, which would provoke immediate arrest rather than risk being subjected to manhandling by the police again [99].

Four days after Black Friday Asquith promised that if the government was returned to office at the forthcoming election it would provide facilities in the next parliament for a bill that could be amended to include women's suffrage. *The Times* interpreted this as meaning that if the Liberal government was re-elected it would be considered to have a mandate for women's suffrage, but the WSPU regarded it as an attempt to postpone reform, since it referred to the next parliament rather than the next session. A WSPU delegation then marched on Downing Street, accosted Asquith, broke his car windows, and injured Augustine Birrell, the Chief Secretary for Ireland. Following this incident, suffragists noted a distinct coolness toward reform among MPs who were suffrage supporters, and the Conciliation Committee temporarily abandoned its efforts to nego-tiate with Asquith [99]. Fawcett was privately angry at the attacks on Asquith because they undermined the NUWSS efforts to build sup-port for reform within the cabinet [*Doc. 17*].

The WSPU's renewed militancy virtually eliminated any possibility that suffrage legislation would be enacted before the First World War. Even suffrage supporters in the government agreed that it could not appear to be giving in to violence. Militancy also turned party opinion against suffrage reform. Following the second reading of the 1912 Conciliation Bill, 34 MPs who had supported reform the year before voted against it; another 70 who had supported it in 1911 ab-stained. Conservative Party conferences voted against suffrage resolutions in 1912 and 1913 despite having supported similar resolu-tions on six occasions prior to 1911 [118].

NEW FORMS OF MILITANCY

Militancy took new forms after 1912 as the WSPU attempted to force the nation to accept that ordinary life could not continue until suf-frage had been granted. Between 1909 and 1912 attacks had concentrated on public property, and the WSPU had been concerned with converting public opinion. After 1912 the WSPU began to at-tack private property and deliberately sought to antagonize public opinion, believing that the public's desire for order would pressure the government into reform [110]. Mrs Pankhurst introduced the new policy of attacks on private property at the October 1912 Albert Hall meeting with the dramatic announcement: 'I incite this meeting to re-bellion' [99 *p. 176*].

During the following two years WSPU militants caused extensive property damage. They burned empty country houses, churches, a school, and post boxes, slashed the *Rokeby Venus* at the National Gallery and exploded a bomb in an unoccupied house Lloyd George was building. It became almost impossible for the WSPU to hold open public meetings because of the attacks on its speakers by angry members of the public.

Although the WSPU is often distinguished from the NUWSS by its use of militant methods, only a minority of WSPU members engaged in militant acts. About 1,000 women were imprisoned for militant acts and some of these were WFL members [131]. Their shared sacri-fices created a sense of sisterhood among those who were imprisoned which lasted for the rest of their lives.

This was especially true of those who were subjected to forced-feeding. In 1909 in order to defeat hunger-striking, the government ordered women to be forcibly fed if they refused to eat. The female prisoner was forcibly held down while a tube was inserted down her throat or nostril and liquid food poured in. In addition to being excruciatingly painful, it involved violation of the woman's body which some considered akin to rape [113] [*Doc. 18*].

Concerned at the public outcry against forced feeding, but fearful that a suffragette might die while on hunger strike and thus become a martyr, the government responded with the 1913 Temporary Discharge for Ill-Health Act. It became known as the Cat-and-Mouse Act because it authorized the government to release a prisoner whose health was endangered by her own actions and then to re-arrest the woman after her health had improved.

Although the government attempted to prevent imprisoned women from dying and becoming martyrs, Emily Davison succeeded in providing the cause with a martyr. In June 1913 she ran onto the Derby course during a race and died after colliding with the king's horse. It is not certain that Davison expected to be killed, but she had stated that the cause needed the 'last consummate sacrifice of the Militant' [110 *p. 138*]. The WSPU had not known of her plan, and did not desire her sacrifice, but used her funeral ceremony as its last public spectacle on behalf of suffrage [110].

The press's distorted images of the suffragettes hampered WSPU efforts to convince the public that their cause was just. Women participating in WSPU demonstrations were repeatedly characterized as 'wild and hysterical' even when this was flagrantly untrue [68 *p. 146*]. Press accounts of Black Friday implied the female demonstrators were responsible for the sexual violence. After 1912 the press focused on 'The Madness of the Militants' seeking to create the impression that they were mentally ill. Anti-suffragist physicians gave credibility to these images of the 'Shrieking Sisterhood' by claiming the women displayed a degree of hysteria as to suggest considerable 'mental disorder' [110 *p. 194*]. The government admitted to requiring medical examinations of imprisoned suffragettes in an unsuccessfull attempt to have them certified as insane.

Although the Pankhursts tolerated male supporters, Christabel informed the all-male Conciliation Committee in 1910: 'This is a women's movement and can only be conducted by women' [69 *p. 26*]. The WSPU's male supporters, such as Henry Brailsford, had persuaded the Pankhursts to support the Conciliation Bill; its collapse in 1911 convinced them not only that the government's promises were worthless, but also that men in general could not be trusted. Their sense of betrayal led to a significant shift in policy in 1912 which included the exclusion of men from the WSPU's campaign [69].

ANTI-MALE POLICIES

The break with the Labour Party in 1912 contributed to the new anti-male policy. In February 1912, Christabel demanded that the Labour Party should stop supporting the Liberal government and vote against them in every division until the Liberals were driven from office. When it refused, Christabel announced: 'A Woman's war upon the Parliamentary Labour Party [became] inevitable' [47 *p. 46*]. By October 1912 the WSPU policy was to attack Labour as well as Liberal candidates in by-elections [99]. The WSPU's continued attacks on the Labour Party weakened Labour support for women's suffrage, and resulted in the Women's Labour League deciding that WSPU membership was incompatible with league membership. League members who belonged to both groups were informed they must resign from either one or the other [40].

Christabel's shift to an anti-male policy also contributed to the expulsion of the Pethick-Lawrences from the WSPU. Before their ouster they had been responsible for much of the WSPU's fundraising, and had donated at least £6,610 of their own money to it between 1906 and 1912 [52]. But they were abruptly dismissed from the WSPU when they resisted Christabel's decision to adopt more violent forms of militancy and urged mass public demonstrations instead [69]. Many WSPU members were shocked by their ouster; some, like Elizabeth Robins, resigned in protest [68].

The Pethick-Lawrences had edited the WSPU's journal, *Votes for Women*, since 1907, and as they retained control of it the split left the WSPU without a journal. Christabel edited the WSPU's new journal, which she surprisingly entitled the *Suffragette*. The term 'suffragette' had been introduced by the *Daily Mail* in 1906 as a derogatory label to distinguish the WSPU from the respectable NUWSS, and WSPU critics had continued to use it in this pejorative sense. Until 1912 the WSPU members called themselves militant suffragists, but Christabel defended the name change on the ground that suffragist implied someone who merely wanted the vote; 'suffragette' indicated someone who was taking action to get it [21].

The WSPU's anti-male sentiment also hampered efforts to work within the existing political system. In November 1912, George Lansbury resigned his parliamentary seat in London's East End in protest against the Labour Party's unwillingness to give priority to women's suffrage over other issues and then campaigned for re-election on the sole issue of votes for women. The WSPU pledged its full support, but its ineptness reduced his chances of success. Public criticism of the Labour Party by Grace Roe, the WSPU's organizer, offended the mainly working-class electorate and generated continuing friction with the local Labour Party. This culminated with the WSPU and the Labour Party refusing to work with each other on election day. The local Labour Party, which lacked cars to transport Lansbury supporters to the polls, refused to provide the WSPU staff with the voting lists which contained the names and addresses of eligible voters, while the WSPU, which had numerous cars available, refused to allow the men to use them claiming: 'Mrs Pankhurst would never allow the Union [WSPU] to work under the men!' [22 *p. 426*]. What was intended as a referendum demonstrating working-class support for women's suffrage instead resulted in a prominent parliamentary suffrage spokesman losing his seat.

After Lansbury's defeat Christabel refused to work with men's organizations and portrayed the campaign as a sex-war against men rather than a struggle with the Liberal government. The public debate on the 1912 White Slave Traffic Bill facilitated the transition to the new approach by drawing attention to male sexual exploitation of women. By portraying itself as leading a moral crusade to defend women against male lust, the WSPU sought to revive its falling membership, increase its revenues and claim the moral authority to resist male power.

WSPU'S NEW IDEOLOGY

Christabel presented the new ideology in a series of articles in 1913 that were republished in pamphlet form as *The Great Scourge and How to End It*. She claimed that male objections to women's suffrage reflected a concern that it would end their sexual exploitation of women. Men feared that if women had the vote they would have the power to end prostitution and the sexual abuse of women. Christabel claimed that 75 to 80 per cent of men were infected with venereal disease before marriage and concluded that women should avoid sexual relations with men. She portrayed the suffrage movement as a revolt against the system under which women were treated as the 'sex slaves of men' and demanded: 'Votes for women and chastity for men' [73 *p. 205*] [*Doc. 19*].

Some suffrage advocates had reservations about Christabel's attempt to use sexuality to mobilize women. Sylvia Pankhurst thought it was intended to stimulate the 'fevered emotions' of the WSPU women who were about to be asked to undertake more serious acts of violence [22 p. 522]. She noted that it enabled the WSPU to draw support across party lines and that it appealed to the Conservative women the WSPU was especially keen to recruit. Feminists seeking to remove restrictions on women's sexual freedom objected because it reinforced the Victorian stereotype of the 'passionless woman' which had contributed to those restrictions. Teresa Billington Greig denounced the Pankhursts for 'feeding and flattering a sexual ideology which juxtaposed the perfection of women against the bestiality of men' [110 p. 224].

Although only women could be WSPU members, prior to 1913 it had numerous male supporters, some of whom made important contributions to the WSPU's campaign [69]. In addition to Frederick Pethick-Lawrence there were others, such as Henry Brailsford and Henry Nevinson, who spoke from WSPU platforms and who were prominent in the Men's Social and Political Union which had been established in 1910 to suppport the WSPU. About 40 men were imprisoned for militant actions undertaken in conjunction with WSPU campaigns; some engaged in hunger strikes and suffered forced feeding [99]. But when Christabel adopted an anti-male policy the Men's Political Union dissolved and its members transferred to other suffrage organizations, such as the United Suffragists.

Following Lansbury's defeat in November 1912, Sylvia developed the WSPU's East London branches into a semi-autonomous organization, the East London Federation of the WSPU (ELF)*. Although ostensibly part of the WSPU it rejected WSPU policy in several areas: it urged universal adult suffrage rather than equal suffrage for women, it did not support the WSPU's arson campaign, and it was not anti-male. In contrast to the WSPU's secret violent acts, the ELF relied on mass public demonstrations, and encouraged its followers to use violence against police who interfered [99].

Sylvia's refusal to accept Christabel's anti-male policy resulted in her expulsion from the WSPU. The divergence between them became an open split in November 1913 when Sylvia appeared on a public platform with Lansbury in violation of Christabel's dictum that WSPU members were not to appear in public meetings with men. Following that meeting Christabel announced in *The Suffragette* that Sylvia was now acting independently of the WSPU. Christabel concluded that 'conflicting views and divided counsels inside the WSPU there cannot be' and therefore it was best that Sylvia go her own way [98 p. 68].

When Sylvia continued to ignore WSPU policy Christabel expelled her from the organization in January 1914. Her reasons included Sylvia's continued co-operation with Lansbury and the Labour movement, the ELF's democratic constitution, the ELF's reliance on working-class women, and Christabel's insistence that all WSPU members were expected to 'take their instructions and walk in step like an army' [22 *p. 517*]. In January 1914 because of Christabel's insistence that the ELF adopt a different name, its members voted to call themselves the East London Federation of the Suffragettes to acknowledge it was no longer part of the WSPU. Its membership was small – only 60 members in May 1914 – but it had much greater importance than this implies because of its close link with the Labour movement's radical wing [98].

Christabel's anti-male policy also contributed to the formation of the United Suffragists. Although its existence was not publicly announced until February 1914, its founders were mainly prominent WSPU members who had been expelled or resigned as a result of Christabel's policy changes. These included the Pethick-Lawrences, Evelyn Sharp, George Lansbury, Henry Nevinson, Hertha Ayrton, Henry Harben, and Gerald Gould, publisher of the *Daily Herald* [99]. In some areas local WSPU branches gave United Suffragists leaders such a warm welcome as to suggest that the Pankhursts could not take their continued loyalty for granted. The United Suffragists was especially important in linking suffrage activists with the syndicalist and radical union campaign which was developing into a mass movement just before the war began [58].

THE ASQUITH INTERVIEW

Asquith met with an ELF deputation in June 1914, on the eve of the First World War. In response to their demand for adult suffrage, Asquith agreed that it would be unjustified to grant limited suffrage to women with unlimited suffrage to men: 'If the change has to come, we must face it boldly and make it thoroughgoing and democratic in its basis' [22 *p. 575*] [*Doc. 20*]. Asquith's reply implied continued opposition to equal votes for women. But it suggested a willingness to accept women's suffrage if it was part of a broader scheme, such as the one eventually adopted in 1918. With a general election expected no later than 1915, and aware that continued resistance might tip enough Liberal voters into the Labour camp to permit a Conservative victory, Asquith's statement and the subsequent negotiations by Lloyd George suggest the Liberal government may have been moving towards an adult-suffrage reform bill [58]. If this is correct, an election pledge of reform was prevented by two developments: the WSPU's refusal to agree to a moratorium on militancy and the outbreak of the First World War.

As Sandra Holton has pointed out, during the last years before the war the WSPU gave priority to the maintenance of militancy over gaining the vote [60]. The struggle against the Liberals had become a kind of holy war, so important that it could not be called off even if continuing it prevented suffrage reform. This preoccupation with the struggle distinguished the WSPU campaign from that by the NUWSS, which remained focused on women's suffrage.

By mid-1914 the WSPU's ability to continue functioning as an effective organization was questionable. In the fiscal year 1912–13 new memberships declined by 34 per cent from the previous year, and in 1913–14 they fell by at least 42 per cent [99]. Large contributions from a few wealthy donors kept the organization's income from falling, but the decline in receipts from meetings and collections suggests diminishing popular support [99]. Finally, the health of many of the activists conducting the militant campaign in 1914 had been impaired by the repeated imprisonments and hunger-strikes, and they could not have continued much longer [61].

When the principle of women's suffrage was conceded in 1918 the Pankhursts insisted the WSPU's prewar campaign had been responsible. Constitutional suffragists disagreed. Eleanor Rathbone* claimed that 'militancy ... came within an inch of wrecking the suffrage movement, perhaps for a generation' and that the outbreak of the war had saved it from destruction by the WSPU [25 *p. 24*].

Historians are also sceptical of WSPU claims that its resort to violence forced the government to concede women's suffrage. Liddington suggests that militant acts 'only attracted public interest, never mass support' [81 *p. 210*]. Harrison and Tickner agree with Rover that suffragette violence after 1912 was 'inadequate to coerce the government but sufficiently destructive to antagonize public opinion' [100 *p. 92*]. Holton concludes that the final stage of militancy involved a 'fundamental failure of political strategy' which served no good purpose in the suffrage campaign [61 *p. 244*], and that it was the pressure from the NUWSS-Labour alliance which was responsible for reform [58].

4 THE NUWSS-LABOUR ALLIANCE, 1910–1914

Between 1910 and 1914 the NUWSS and the WSPU moved in opposite directions. While the WSPU's social base was narrowing and its politics becoming increasingly Conservative, the NUWSS became a mass movement with formal ties to the Labour Party. Although in its early years the NUWSS was open to the charge that it was a 'bourgeois' women's movement, after 1910 its support from working-class women increased significantly. The NUWSS's expansion during the period was dramatic: from 210 affiliated societies in 1910 to over 500 by July 1914, from 21,571 members in 1910 to over 100,000 members or Friends of Women's Suffrage in 1914, and an increase in annual revenues from £5,500 in 1910 to over £45,000 in 1914 [62].

By 1910 a majority of the House of Commons supported women's suffrage, but party differences as to what form it should take blocked legislation. Conservatives supported equal suffrage rights, but Liberals opposed this because those enfranchised would be propertied women who would be likely to vote Conservative. Liberals preferred to include women in a measure which would expand the male electorate but Conservatives resisted this since the new voters would be mainly Liberal or Labour supporters. The Conciliation Committee was established in 1910 to draft a bill acceptable to both Liberals and Conservatives. Chaired by the Earl of Lytton, a Conservative and the brother of the WSPU militant, Lady Constance Lytton, the committee included 54 MPs from all parties and was supported by both the NUWSS and the WSPU.

The Conciliation Committee drafted a very narrow bill that was intended to give the parliamentary vote to those women who were local government electors. Because it restricted the vote primarily to single women householders, it would have enfranchised only about a million women. Fearful that these would be largely Tory-voting elderly spinsters and widows, David Lloyd George and Winston Churchill voted against the Conciliation Bill, but it passed its second reading by a vote of 299 to 189 [99]. Although the government refused to provide additional time in that parliamentary session, it did promise to allow time for further consideration of a suffrage bill in the next.

THE CONCILIATION BILL

In 1911 a modified Conciliation Bill was introduced which revived optimism that legislation would be passed. In order to demonstrate broad public support for the bill the NUWSS urged its affiliated societies to lobby local councils to endorse it: 146 town, county and district councils passed resolutions supporting the bill which were forwarded to parliament [62]. The new Conciliation Bill passed its second reading with an even larger majority than the 1910 bill: 255 to 88. Sensing victory, the NUWSS then lobbied the government to grant parliamentary time for the bill to proceed. Their hopes were dashed, however, as a divided Cabinet refused, but offered a week in the next session if a similar bill could again pass its second reading. The NUWSS suspected duplicity, but Asquith publicly pledged that the government would ensure that adequate time would be allowed in the next session for the bill [62].

Although the NUWSS desired legislation granting women the vote on the same terms as men, they continued to support the Conciliation Bill because they believed a wider bill could not secure a parliamentary majority unless it was a government sponsored measure and this seemed impossible given Asquith's opposition. But just when it appeared the government would allow a Conciliation Bill to pass through parliament Lloyd George intervened.

Lloyd George was among the Liberal suffragists who sought the defeat of the Conciliation bills. He was convinced that they would add 'hundreds of thousands' of Tory voters to the electorate because of the qualifications for enfranchisement [99]. In response to Lloyd George's concern, the Liberal Party chief whip conducted a survey of the provincial Liberal federations which revealed that Liberal Party agents were almost unanimously opposed to the Conciliation Bill. There was some support, however, for granting all women the vote [99, 87].

During the latter part of 1911 Lloyd George developed an alternative to the Conciliation Bill: a government franchise bill drafted to allow women's suffrage amendments to be added to it. Anticipating that this would grant the vote to working-class women who were likely to be Liberal voters, Lloyd George urged suffragists to reject the Conciliation Bill. On 7 November 1911 Asquith informed a

People's Suffrage Federation deputation that the government intended to introduce a reform bill which could be amended to include women's suffrage, that the government would not oppose such amendments and that it would ensure that the bill passed through all its stages in 1912 [62]. Suffrage reformers were divided by these proposals. By holding out the possibility of a wider measure of reform it encouraged those who preferred this to repudiate the Conciliation Bill. Some reformers believed this was not only the consequence of Asquith's announcement, but his intention as well [110].

Although they believed the government's franchise bill had a better chance of success, the NUWSS continued to urge enactment of the Conciliation Bill. But the WSPU revived large-scale militant action prior to the vote on it. In reaction to the WSPU violence, constituency support for women's suffrage declined and MPs who had expressed support began to waver. Even though the 1912 Conciliation Bill was essentially the same as the one passed by a large majority in 1911, it was defeated by a vote of 222 to 208. A relieved Asquith informed the Liberal chief whip: 'I think we are now nearly out of the wood' [87 *p. 99*]. The defeat was due in part to the withdrawal of Irish Nationalist support, but 26 Liberal and Conservative MPs who had pledged to support the bill (many of whom had voted for the 1911 bill) voted against it, and 66 who had abstained in 1911 voted against it. The NUWSS believed WSPU militancy was responsible for this [62].

THE LIBERAL PARTY'S BEHAVIOUR

NUWSS leaders felt betrayed by the Liberal Party's behaviour during the vote on the Conciliation Bill; this feeling was strengthened by the collapse of its franchise bill. Despite the government's pledge that the bill had been drafted in such a manner as to permit a women's suffrage amendment, when it was under consideration in January 1913, the Speaker of the House of Commons ruled it out of order. This was surprising in that the bill had been drafted with the intent that it should be amended, and women's suffrage amendments to the Franchise Bills of 1867 and 1884 had been permitted. The Speaker's impartiality has been questioned. James Lowther was a Conservative who personally opposed women's suffrage, and who had spent the weekend before making his ruling at the home of Lord Rothschild, a leading financial contributor to the anti-suffrage cause. It is not clear whether Asquith anticipated the Speaker's ruling, but in a private letter he expressed his satisfaction: 'The Speaker's *coup d'etat* has bowled over the Women for the session – a great relief' [112 *p. 207*].

Women Liberals were especially demoralized by the Liberal government's handling of the suffrage issue. Resignations by Women's Liberal Federation leaders were commonplace, and the rank-and-file membership shrank rapidly. After increasing from 66,000 to 133,215 between 1904 and 1912, WLF membership declined to 121,888 in the following year. One local WFL member reported: 'Every bright and clever woman in my [local] Liberal society has left us' [58 *p. 119*].

Prior to 1912 the majority of NUWSS members were Liberals, and it had always assumed that women's suffrage would be established by the Liberal Party. But the Liberal government's handling of the issue discredited this assumption, and led the NUWSS to change its strategy. Two groups within the NUWSS pressed for an alternative strategy involving an electoral alliance with the Labour Party but viewed that alliance in very different terms. One, led by Fawcett, saw it as a temporary expedient which would be abandoned once the Liberal Party had been forced to include women's suffrage in its programme. A second group, the democratic suffragists, considered the Labour Party to be feminism's natural ally and intended that the alliance should become a permanent link.

Pressure within the NUWSS for an alliance with the Labour Party came primarily from branches in the north of England and Scotland. The Newcastle Society, led by Dr Ethel Bentham, a Fabian Socialist and a member of the Women's Labour League, was the strongest advocate of this policy and was backed by the Manchester and Edinburgh suffrage societies. With Kathleen Courtney as secretary and Margaret Robertson as organiser, the Manchester Society made special efforts to recruit working-class women and worked for pro-suffrage Labour Party candidates in by-elections prior to 1912 [58].

The NUWSS women urging an alliance with Labour represented a younger generation drawn from the provinces. After 1909 they began to occupy positions of authority within the NUWSS. Kathleen Courtney became the NUWSS secretary in 1910; Catherine Marshall became parliamentary secretary in 1911; Helena Swanwick was the editor of the NUWSS journal, *Common Cause*, from its establishment in 1909, and she, along with Margaret Aston and Ethel Bentham, became NUWSS executive committee members between 1909 and 1912. The employment of working-class women organisers such as Ada Nield Chew and Selina Cooper strengthened the links with Labour [58]. Thus, by 1912 the mainly southern, middle-class, Liberal women who had directed the NUWSS since its inception were being replaced by women who had closer ties with northern working-class women and the Labour Party.

Until 1912 Fawcett and her allies on the NUWSS executive blocked an alliance with the Labour Party. But the desertion of many supposed Liberal suffrage supporters in the 1912 parliamentary vote which defeated the Conciliation Bill dealt the 'fatal shock' to the NUWSS's traditional policy. It demonstrated that Liberal MPs were not reliable suffrage supporters as long as their party was not committed to reform. Almost immediately Fawcett reversed her position and began to explore the possibility of an alliance with Labour.

LABOUR PARTY ALLIANCE

The Labour Party appealed to the NUWSS in part because it had a stronger record of support for women's suffrage than any other party. In contrast to the Liberals, all the Labour MPs present had voted for the Conciliation Bill. Also, at its January 1912 annual conference the Labour Party made women's suffrage part of its programme and pledged that it would not accept any franchise reform which did not include women.

While an electoral alliance with Labour offered the NUWSS some advantages, it also created new tensions. Fawcett did not intend to abandon the NUWSS's traditional non-party position, but a link with Labour, even if limited to supporting Labour candidates in by-elections, aroused concern among some Liberal and Conservative NUWSS members that the NUWSS was altering its non-party stance. The Labour Party's association with socialism was a further problem. Fawcett and her associates were aware that the vast majority of NUWSS members were middle-class women who were hostile to Labour's programme on issues other than suffrage. If forced to choose between loyalty to their class and loyalty to women's suffrage, Fawcett anticipated they would give priority to their class interests and abandon the suffrage movement [62].

Because of these concerns, Fawcett and Catherine Marshall went to great lengths to deny that the agreement with Labour was a fundamental shift in NUWSS policy. Fawcett presented it as a temporary policy based on political expediency. Privately she assured NUWSS members that once the Liberal Party made women's suffrage part of its programme the Labour connection would be abandoned [62]. Marshall informed NUWSS members that the policy was intended to attack anti-suffrage Liberal MPs and should not be construed as an alliance with Labour. In an attempt to defuse Liberal women's opposition, Marshall also promised that the policy would be administered by a special committee and would be financed from a fund kept separate from other NUWSS funds so that those who disliked the new scheme would not have to contribute to its support [58].

Urged on by the Newcastle and Manchester societies, Fawcett convened a special meeting of the NUWSS council in May 1912 to consider an electoral alliance with Labour. Although many Liberal women were so disillusioned with the Liberal government's behaviour over the Conciliation Bill that they were prepared to support action injurious to their party, a minority were not. Within the NUWSS executive the strongest opposition came from Eleanor Rathbone who warned Fawcett before the meeting that the scheme risked alienating pro-suffrage Liberals; she was also one of three women who spoke against the proposal at the meeting. Despite her objections the council agreed: (1) that when deciding whom to support in an election the NUWSS would take into account the position of the parties involved as well as that of the individual candidates; (2) that Labour candidates should be supported especially in constituencies currently represented by Liberals with an unsatisfactory record on suffrage; and (3) that a fund be established for the purpose of carrying out this election policy [112].

The new policy met with considerable support. Within four months after it was adopted over £4,300 had been raised for Labour candidates. It drew WSPU supporters such as Lady de la Warr and Henry N. Brailsford into the NUWSS. It also led other suffrage organizations to adopt similar policies: the WFL and the Men's League for Women's Suffrage also decided to support Labour candidates in three-cornered contests. Although Ramsay MacDonald was ambivalent, other Labour Party leaders welcomed the NUWSS initiative, in part because the 1911 Osborne judgement had reduced the funds available to the party for election expenses [58].

THE ELECTION FIGHTING FUND COMMITTEE

The NUWSS established the Election Fighting Fund Committee* (EFF) to implement the new policy and administer its funds. The EFF was responsible to the NUWSS executive and initially it included eight executive committee members. As might be expected, the original committee was heavily weighted with democratic suffragists who had northern connections: Margaret Ashton, Kathleen Courtney, Isabella Ford, Ethel Snowden and Catherine Marshall, its secretary, among others.

When the council created the EFF it also established a related scheme called the Friends of Women's Suffrage. Intended to increase the number of working-class women supporting women's suffrage, it allowed persons who could not afford NUWSS dues to enrol as a 'friend' of women's suffrage by signing a card expressing approval of women's right to vote. Once enrolled, participants were invited to suffrage meetings and provided with suffrage literature. By the outbreak of the First World War 39,500 Friends of Women's Suffrage had enrolled, substantially increasing the largely middle-class NUWSS's links with the working class during the period that the alliance with Labour was being developed [58, 62].

The EFF participated in four by-elections in 1912 and succeeded in reducing the number of Liberal MPs, thereby making the Liberal government more dependent on the Labour Party. Although the Liberal candidate won re-election at the Holmfirth by-election in June, the NUWSS considered its intervention successful. Even though the constituency was solidly Liberal, the Liberal candidate's majority was reduced by one-half, and the Labour vote almost doubled. In the Crewe and Midlothian by-elections later that year the Liberal vote was reduced sufficiently to transform the two Liberal seats into Conservative majorities. In both cases the Labour candidate polled well in constituencies Labour had not contested in the last general election. The Hanley by-election was less successful, but the Labour candidate's poor performance reflected the lack of Labour organization in the constituency rather than the EFF's work.

The EFF's electoral activity impressed both Labour and Liberal Party leaders. Labour leaders were pleased with the EFF's contribution in all four elections, but singled out its role at Midlothian for special praise. The Labour Party's chief agent credited the EFF with adding 1,000 votes to the Labour total there and with having been a significant factor in the Liberal defeat. A Liberal Party whip informed Catherine Marshall privately that the EFF's by-election work was causing great concern within the Liberal Party. The *Manchester Guardian* calculated that if the Midlothian trends continued the result would be a Conservative majority at the next general election [62].

At the executive's request, the February 1913 NUWSS council passed several resolutions expanding the EFF's scope. It decided not to support any government candidate, no matter how reliable he was on the suffrage issue, although a 'tried friend' would not be actively opposed. It agreed to attack the seats of anti-suffragist Liberals, especially those who were ministers, at the next general election. Support would be given to either Labour or Unionist candidates for this purpose. Also, the executive was now authorized to transfer money from the union's general fund to the EFF which previously had been prohibited. These decisions strengthened the EFF and moved the NUWSS further towards an anti-Liberal Party policy [112, 58].

During 1913 women from northern suffrage societies pressed for stronger Labour Party ties. The November 1913 NUWSS council meeting considered a resolution from the Newcastle society intended to increase the number of constituencies in which the EFF would do election work in preparation for the approaching general election. The EFF policy at that time was to concentrate on constituencies in which there were especially important anti-suffrage Liberals or especially pro-suffrage Labour candidates. The resolution proposed that securing the return of the largest number of Labour candidates should be the EFF's goal, and that to this end it should place less importance on the views of the individual candidates than on the strength of the local Labour vote and the smallness of the Liberal majority. But even some of the strongest proponents of the Labour alliance, such as Catherine Marshall, opposed this resolution because it committed the NUWSS to support the Labour Party in the general election. While she agreed the NUWSS should adopt this approach at the election if the Liberal Party did not include women's suffrage in its programme, Marshall thought it more effective to keep this as a threat which could be used to pressure the Liberals. Despite Marshall's opposition the resolution was only narrowly defeated (by ten votes), an indication that pro-Labour sentiment was increasing within the NUWSS [112, 58].

In 1913–14 the EFF intervened in four by-elections on behalf of Labour candidates. Although Labour did not win any of the seats, this was unsurprising since Labour was contesting three of the constituencies for the first time. The NUWSS considered the by-elections to have been successful in that the Liberals lost two seats which they previously had held, and in the other two their majority was substantially reduced. Also, a Labour organization was established in each constituency upon which the Labour candidate could build at the general election.

The relationship between the NUWSS and the Labour movement may have begun as a short-term electoral policy based on expediency, but by 1914 it was growing beyond this. In response to reports circulating within the Labour Party that the NUWSS intended to oppose Labour candidates at the next general election (due no later than 1915), the NUWSS executive sent a deputation to the January 1914

ILP executive meeting to explain what NUWSS policy would be if the Liberal Party included suffrage in its general election programme. It pledged that if this occurred the NUWSS would not continue its present opposition to the Liberal Party, but that it would not abandon its current commitments to Labour candidates, nor would it oppose any Labour candidate provided that the candidate's personal attitude towards women's suffrage was satisfactory [58].

REVOLT AGAINST EFF POLICY

Although this reassured the ILP, it triggered a revolt within the NUWSS executive. Eleanor Rathbone, who had raised objections to the EFF scheme at the February 1913 council meeting [*Doc. 21*], led the revolt, claiming that the statement altered NUWSS policy and had not been approved by the NUWSS council. She was convinced that it required the union to support the Labour Party in the forthcoming general election. Rathbone believed this would split the progressive vote and very likely result in the formation of a Conservative government which would never introduce women's suffrage [112, 62].

Presumably at Rathbone's request, the Liverpool suffrage society submitted a resolution for the next council meeting seeking to prevent the EFF from working in any constituency where the outcome was likely to be the election of a Conservative candidate. Within the NUWSS executive Catherine Marshall led the resistance to the Liverpool resolution as she recognized that it would mortally weaken the EFF. While she acknowledged that a Conservative government would also be risky, she remained convinced that the return of a Liberal government with no definite pledge on women's suffrage was the greatest danger. In her view, the EFF was not simply an anti-Liberal strategy, but a scheme to purge reform opponents from that party. The executive endorsed her position by voting eleven to two against the Liverpool resolution [112].

The depth of Rathbone's hostility toward the EFF policy is suggested by her decision to initiate an opposition movement rather than accept the executive's decision. Shortly after the executive voted against the Liverpool resolution, Rathbone sent out a letter suggesting that delegates to the forthcoming NUWSS council meeting from societies which did not support the union's 'Anti-Government policy' should meet to plan concerted action on this matter. A meeting was held and a committee elected to organize opposition to the executive's policy at the forthcoming council meeting. Members of the executive were stunned when they became aware of this. Dissidents

were entitled to confer informally, but establishing a formal committee to direct opposition to an executive decision seemed disloyal; the
fact that Rathbone's initial steps were taken secretly suggests she realized this. Rathbone's action also violated the principle that members
of the executive, like the Cabinet, were obligated to support majority
decisions. Fawcett was so alarmed that she wrote to Rathbone expressing her concern that Rathbone's behaviour, if imitated by others,
would necessarily lead to the 'break up of the Union' [112 *p. 326*].

The executive committee attempted to resolve the revolt initiated
by Rathbone and her three supporters on the executive at its March
1914 meeting. Although there were other Liberal women on the executive who must have had reservations about the closer ties with
Labour, Rathbone was unable to attract additional support. By a vote
of twelve to four the executive decided that any attempt to organize
support or opposition for any course of action at the general election
before a special council had been called to consider the matter 'must
inevitably damage the present effectiveness of the Union's policy, and
thus stultify the decisions of the Council' [112 *p. 327*]. A further resolution was passed without opposition calling for a special council
meeting to consider the matter.

The issues of election policy and appropriate behaviour by executive committee members were both thrashed out at the April 1914
council meeting. When it upheld the executive committee's position
and voted a special resolution of thanks to Catherine Marshall for
her effective defence of the EFF policy, Rathbone and her three supporters on the executive committee resigned from the executive.
Privately Rathbone continued to insist that there was widespread dis-
content with the union's 'Labour policy' and that the council's action
had been a series of votes of confidence in Fawcett's leadership rather
than a true reflection of opinion on the issues [112, 102].

Despite the concerns of Liberal women, the NUWSS continued its
efforts to reduce the Liberal majority at the next general election, and
to ensure that, if another Liberal government was formed, it would
be dependent on the support of a Labour Party committed to
women's suffrage. During 1913–14 the EFF increased its activity in
the constituencies of five Liberal anti-suffrage ministers; it canvassed
and registered voters and assisted Labour in developing a local organization where it was weak. The NUWSS also urged the Labour Party
to contest these seats at the general election with candidates who
were strong suffrage supporters; by 1914 Labour had agreed to do so
in three of the constituencies.

DIVISIONS WITHIN THE NUWSS

Divisions continued within the NUWSS over EFF policy, and with the approach of the general election the danger of a split increased. The issue of how the EFF would be used in the general election generated much of the tension. Although many Liberal women accepted its use to support Labour candidates in a small number of constituencies contested by anti-suffrage Liberals, the proposal to expand the EFF beyond this was another matter. With a general election near, party loyalty began to replace the anger which Liberal women had felt towards their party's handling of the suffrage issue in 1912. Holton concludes that if the NUWSS had honoured its commitment to the Labour Party at the general election there would have been a 'serious rebellion' by rank and file Liberal women within the NUWSS. Certainly it is true that the approach of the general election was heightening the tension between the NUWSS leaders who supported the EFF as a short-term policy of expediency and the democratic suffragists who thought it was the dawn of a natural alliance between feminist and class politics [58].

Aware that its attacks on Liberal candidates could result in a Conservative government at the next general election, during 1913–14 the NUWSS intensified its efforts to obtain a pledge from the Conservative Party that it would introduce a suffrage bill if it formed a government. By 1914 support for women's suffrage within the Conservative Party had increased significantly. The 1911 National Union of Conservative and Unionist Associations' annual conference endorsed the Conciliation Bill, and both Balfour and Andrew Bonar Law supported it. In mid-July 1914 the NUWSS was preparing to announce that Arthur Steel-Maitland, the Conservative Party chairman, had converted to women's suffrage [58]. While anti-suffragists were able to obtain names and other assistance from Liberal Party agents, they found Conservative agents unhelpful [89]. The growing support within the Conservative Party reflected an awareness that the party would benefit from reform; party leaders calculated that the one million female voters who would be enfranchised by the Conciliation Bill would substantially increase Conservative electoral prospects and reacted accordingly.

Concerned that the Conservative Party would make women's suffrage an election issue by endorsing reform, the Liberal government appears to have become convinced during 1914 that it had to do something in order to prevent the Conservatives from seizing the issue and using it to their electoral benefit. Asquith, whose opposition had previously prevented the Liberal government from acting, met with an East London Federation of Suffragettes deputation in June 1914, and indicated that he was prepared to accept women's suffrage provided it was 'democratic in its basis' [*58 p. 124*] – i.e., that suffrage reform include working-class women, a majority of whom could be expected to vote Liberal. After the meeting, with Asquith's approval, Lloyd George began negotiations with Sylvia Pankhurst and George Lansbury. The WSPU's revival of militancy ended this promising development, but it is part of the reason why Sandra Holton and Jo Vellacott believe the Liberal Party would have committed itself to suffrage reform before the 1915 election if the First World War had not intervened [58, 112].

5 WAR AND SUFFRAGE REFORM, 1914–18

Although the principle of women's suffrage was conceded in 1918, historians disagree as to whether the First World War was the cause or simply the occasion for reform. As munitions workers and in other roles, women made a vital contribution to the war effort. This led some historians to claim that women gained the vote as a reward for their performance on the home front. But this interpretation is undermined by the fact that only women aged 30 and above were granted the vote in 1918, whereas most munitions workers, and indeed the great majority of all women war workers, were under 30.

What the war did do was to remove the main obstacles to reform. Prior to 1914 women's suffrage was blocked by Asquith's opposition, WSPU militancy, and party conflict over what form legislation should take. During the war all three were removed: the WSPU abandoned militancy; Asquith resigned as prime minister in 1916; and the formation of a coalition government removed the issue from overt party politics. The war also provided suffragists with the opportunity to support the use of physical force in defence of their country and the empire, thus undermining one of the anti-suffragists' main arguments.

SUFFRAGISTS AND THE PEACE MOVEMENT

When they realized that Britain might be drawn into the war, most suffragists, including the NUWSS, considered it a disaster and sought to restore the peace. The NUWSS participated in the women's peace rally on 4 August organized by the Women's Labour League and the Women's Co-operative Guild intended to support British neutrality but, by the time it was held, Germany had invaded Belgium and a British declaration of war on Germany was expected within hours. Many women at the meeting were frustrated by a situation that they attributed to an inherent male proclivity for violence. Desperately seeking some means of restoring peace, the participants unanimously passed a resolution urging neutral nations to mediate an end to the war [116].

Fawcett, who chaired the meeting, urged the women to recognize their duty to support their country in the crisis. Although Fawcett's statements were patriotic, because the meeting had originally been advertised as a peace rally, the press portrayed it as part of a women's peace initiative [116].

The meeting revived male fears that women could not be trusted with the vote because they would be pacifists. On the following day Lord Robert Cecil, one of the Conservative Party's most important suffrage advocates, warned Fawcett that by participating in a peace meeting and allowing the NUWSS to be involved in promoting it, she had shaken his belief 'in the fitness of women to deal with great Imperial questions . . . ' [72 *p. 76*]. He warned that the NUWSS risked losing its supporters in the Conservative and Liberal Parties if she took further action along those lines [*Doc. 22*]. Convinced that suffrage could not be obtained without the support of allies like Cecil, Fawcett announced in the *Common Cause* the following week: 'Let us show ourselves worthy of citizenship whether our claim to it be recognized or not' [102 *p. 214*].

Confronted with a choice between a peace policy based upon sexual difference ideology or a policy which would increase the chances of gaining women's suffrage, Fawcett chose the latter. But, while the NUWSS executive agreed to suspend the suffrage campaign temporarily, it was divided as to what policy it should take towards the war. Some members of the executive wanted the NUWSS to support the peace movement. Believing that the underlying goal of the women's movement was to gain the vote in order to help establish the supremacy of reason over physical force, Helena Swanwick was convinced that if women did not work for peace the moral basis of their movement would be eroded [31]. Shortly after the Union of Democratic Control was established in September 1914 to work for a negotiated peace, Swanwick joined and began recruiting other NUWSS women: Isabella Ford, Margaret (Robertson) Hills, Ethel Snowden and Ethel Williams were among those who became members [31].

But many NUWSS members opposed any association with the peace movement. It would expose the women's suffrage movement to the charge that it was disloyal in wartime and eliminate any possibility of gaining the vote in the foreseeable future. Lady Francis Balfour maintained that German aggression caused the war and insisted there should be no talk of peace until Germany was defeated. Some who held this view considered the war analogous to domestic violence: Germany was portrayed as the powerful male aggressor, Belgium and Britain as the vulnerable female victims of male violence, and the war as an attempt by the international community to protect the rights of the weak against the physically strong [72].

NUWSS critics of the war divided into two groups, both opposed to Fawcett's position. One, led by Swanwick and Ford, urged the NUWSS to sponsor an anti-war campaign. A second group, which included Kathleen Courtney, Catherine Marshall, and Margaret Ashton, sympathized with Swanwick's position but feared it would split the NUWSS. Seeking to avoid this, they proposed that the NUWSS conduct an educational campaign on the causes and prevention of war. Most democratic suffragists belonged to these two groups [58].

Although they differed as to what tactics to follow, suffragists who wished the NUWSS to work for peace shared a conviction that the suffrage campaign's purpose was not simply to expand the electorate. Underlying their sexual difference ideology was an assumption that women were morally superior to men and that therefore women would use the franchise differently from men. They desired women's suffrage because they expected it to transform society. Part of this transformation involved the substitution of moral for physical force. The idea of granting women equal political rights while retaining male institutions and values seemed like a betrayal of the principles that had made the women's suffrage movement something akin to a moral crusade. This conviction that the vote would be meaningless if the suffrage movement simply sought equal rights in a man-made world is reflected in Maude Royden's warning that for women 'to ask for equal rights with men in a world governed by . . . [physical] force is frivolous' [31, *p. 42*].

Within a few weeks after Britain entered the war the NUWSS was engaged in an acrimonious struggle to determine what position it should take. Initially the Courtney-Marshall group was successful. They defeated Fawcett's proposed resolution for the November 1914 provincial council's agenda. When the council met it approved resolutions supported by the Courtney-Marshall group calling for an educational campaign 'to keep public opinion sane' [58 *p. 135*], for a European partnership based upon equal rights in place of reliance upon force and for the *Common Cause* to publish articles on the causes and prevention of war. Although provincial councils could not set NUWSS policy, these resolutions indicated strong NUWSS support for the Courtney-Marshall position [58].

DIVISIONS WITHIN THE NUWSS

Courtney and Marshall hoped that Fawcett would accept their compromise position in order to avoid splitting the NUWSS. But in the following months Fawcett and her opponents became irreconcilable. Each side believed its position reflected a woman's view of the war. Fawcett informed the council that the British Empire was at war to preserve democracy against Prussian authoritarianism, and warned that a Prussian victory would make it even more difficult to obtain women's suffrage. Anti-war members, such as Maude Royden, claimed the women's movement was an attempt to assert the supremacy of spiritual over physical force, and therefore the NUWSS should seek a negotiated peace [102].

The division within the NUWSS was so fundamental that a split probably could not have been avoided. But Fawcett did little to prevent it. One issue precipitating the rift was a proposal that the International Women's Suffrage Alliance (IWSA) business congress meet in a neutral country in 1915. Fawcett strongly opposed this, fearing the meeting would become the focus of a 'women for peace' movement but when the issue came before the NUWSS executive only one other member supported her. Rather than accepting the majority vote, Fawcett wrote to Carrie Chapman Catt, the IWSA president, threatening to resign her position as the IWSA's first vice-president if they went ahead with it.

The NUWSS's internal conflict came to a head at the February 1915 annual council meeting. Initially the internationalists were successful. Resolutions they supported were passed urging Catt to convene an IWSA meeting in a neutral country (despite Fawcett's speaking against it), recommending an educational campaign on the causes of war and proposing: 'Since the Women's Movement is based on the principle that social relations should be governed not by physical force but by recognition of mutual rights' the NUWSS 'declares its belief in arbitration' and urges that 'future International disputes shall be submitted to arbitration ... before recourse is had to military force ... ' [116 *p. 70*; 72 *p. 78*].

But these expressions of support for the internationalists were undermined by other developments that left them feeling defeated. The council rejected a resolution committing the NUWSS to implementing the above resolutions. It also passed a resolution Fawcett desired pledging the NUWSS to work aimed at 'the sustaining of the vital strength of the nation' [102 *p. 217*], which her group interpreted as supporting the war effort. Finally, on the last day of the council meeting, Fawcett made a belligerent speech in which she stated that until German troops had been driven from French and Belgian soil: 'I believe it is akin to treason to talk of peace' [116 *p. 71*].

The internationalists were stunned by Fawcett's public declaration that she considered them traitors and the first wave of resignations followed soon afterwards. Maude Royden resigned as *Common Cause* editor, and Kathleen Courtney and Catherine Marshall, the NUWSS's most important officers after Fawcett, resigned their respective positions as honorary secretary and parliamentary secretary [*Doc. 23*]. By April 1915, 12 of the 24 executive committee members had resigned. Fawcett never forgave them; three years later she described them privately as 'base and treacherous children who would fain stab her [England] in the back in her moment of peril' [102 *p. 221*].

Despite the February council's vote supporting an international women's conference, at its March meeting the NUWSS executive committee decided not to participate. Fawcett insisted the NUWSS's reputation would be damaged if it was associated with the meeting, since it would inevitably involve discussions of a negotiated peace. Lady Francis Balfour warned that if the NUWSS participated in the congress she would leave the NUWSS and initiate a campaign against the internationalists. Despite Isabella Ford's insistence that the suffrage cause was necessarily opposed to militarism, the executive voted eleven to five against sending delegates to the congress [72].

The June 1915 special council was a victory for Fawcett's group. The council passed a vote of confidence in her, and a new slate of officers who supported Fawcett was elected to replace the internationalists. Ray Strachey, Fawcett's close friend and political ally, became parliamentary secretary. The election significantly changed the political make-up of the NUWSS executive: the internationalist and pro-Labour majority was replaced by a pro-war and anti-Labour majority.

The NUWSS's alliance with Labour through the Election Fighting Fund was one of the split's casualties. After the war began Fawcett changed her position on the EFF, maintaining that the EFF policy should be abandoned so that if a wartime general election was held the NUWSS would be free to support the government. Strachey, a Conservative, sought to terminate the EFF once she became parliamentary secretary. At its May 1915 meeting the executive concluded that the February council's resolution suspending all political work implied suspending EFF activity. At this point Marshall and Margaret (Robertson) Hills resigned from the EFF Committee; the rest of the democratic suffragists followed suit shortly afterwards.

The Labour Party was informed in August 1915 that the NUWSS was suspending its EFF policy, and in 1918, prior to the general election, it was definitely terminated [58].

The NUWSS's decision to avoid any association with the peace movement was crucial to obtaining women's suffrage during the war. Part of the anti-suffragist case rested on the belief that women were more inclined to pacifism than men and thus could not be trusted to support their country in wartime. If the NUWSS had supported efforts to develop links with women from enemy nations, or had encouraged an anti-war movement in Britain, it is highly unlikely that women's suffrage would have been granted prior to the war's end. The treatment of conscientious objectors supports this point; they were deprived of the franchise for five years after the war for refusing to support the war effort [130, 116].

In contrast to the two larger suffrage organizations, the Women's Freedom League continued to campaign for the suffrage after the war began. Aware that suffragists might be pulled away from the reform effort by patriotic feelings, the WFL urged them not to abandon the campaign: 'we make a strong appeal to all Suffragists to stand to their guns and man their own forts and not to let themselves be drawn out of their Movement for any purpose whatsoever' [72 *p. 155*]. The WFL viewed the war as the unnecessary but logical outcome of a man-made world based on physical force; the conflict thus demonstrated the supreme importance of women having a voice in political affairs [47]. Although Charlotte Despard, the WFL President, was a prominent pacifist, the WFL did not endorse her position; in 1917 it issued a public warning that Despard's anti-war activities reflected her individual beliefs rather than WFL policy [88].

THE WSPU AND THE WAR

The war brought an end to the WSPU as a suffrage organization. When the war began Christabel Pankhurst denounced it as a man-made conflict which was 'God's vengeance' upon those who held women in subjection. But when the government released the suffragette prisoners a few days later Mrs Pankhurst ordered suffrage activity suspended. She and Christabel developed a gendered rationale for an increasingly chauvinistic view of the conflict. Denouncing Germany as a 'male nation', they urged Britons to come to the defence of France, a 'feminine' state which they claimed was the victim of male aggression. Although the other suffrage societies joined together in 1916 to resume working for women's suffrage, the WSPU continued to focus on the war and did not participate in the revived suffrage campaign [61].

The WSPU's new policy shocked some of its former supporters. In light of the prewar expectation that women would stand for peace, Sylvia Pankhurst considered it a betrayal of the women's movement [22]. In October 1915, Rose Lamartine Yates chaired a meeting of dissident WSPU members who objected to the WSPU's transformation from a suffrage to a pro-war organization. WSPU members who wished to dissociate themselves from Mrs Pankhurst's wartime policy established two breakaway organizations in 1916: the Suffragettes of the WSPU and the Independent WSPU [99].

Under Sylvia Pankhurst's direction, the East London Federation of Suffragettes became an important centre of anti-war activity which brought her into close contact with adult suffragists in anti-war organizations. During the early years of the war she began to see the struggle more as a class than a gender conflict, and in March 1916 she changed the name of the ELFS to the Workers' Suffrage Federation to reflect this new focus [117].

It has been claimed that the women's suffrage movement was moribund until the government revived the issue of franchise reform late in 1916, but this is misleading. During the first half of 1916 suffrage societies debated whether to seek adult suffrage or women's suffrage. At a suffrage conference in January 1916, Sylvia Pankhurst's motion for full adult suffrage was supported by the United Suffragists, the Women's Freedom League, and by some NUWSS members. Two months later 23 suffrage societies established a consultative committee chaired by Eleanor Rathbone to work for women's suffrage. While its members remained divided as to their goal, adult suffrage proponents were prominent [31]. Thus, when the government took up franchise reform late in 1916, a limited measure of women's suffrage was the least radical among the reform proposals that suffrage groups were seeking.

FRANCHISE REFORM

The suffrage issue was revived in 1916 because the possibility of a general election forced the government to reform the law to enable men in the armed forces to vote. The existing requirements included a residence qualification which would have disqualified most of the men serving in the military. The introduction of conscription in 1916 made suffrage reform even more imperative. But some Cabinet members believed that if franchise reform was introduced, something would have to be done about women's suffrage. Arthur Henderson was an important force for reform within the Cabinet; he insisted that only adult suffrage would reconcile the working class to conscription. Aware of the strong resistance to any reform that would make women a majority of the electorate, Henderson suggested that women be enfranchised at age 25, and claimed this was acceptable to the women's organizations [87].

Fawcett also made it clear that the NUWSS's wartime quiescence would end if the government were to introduce franchise reform that did not include women: 'they [NUWSS] had buried the hatchet, but they had marked the place where it was buried and were prepared if occasion arose to dig it up' [81 *p. 81*]. Encouraged by Henderson and Lord Robert Cecil, Fawcett wrote to the prime minister to remind him that any legislation he might be contemplating should not prejudice the prospects for women's suffrage. Asquith replied that there was no plan for altering the franchise at present, but assured her that if this should be undertaken 'the considerations set out in your letter will be fully and impartially weighed without any pre-judgement from the controversies of the past' [58 *p. 146*]. Fawcett recognized that the opportunity for reform had emerged and ordered the NUWSS organization into action. Ministers were soon inundated with correspondence insisting that any franchise reform should include women's suffrage [89].

During the following months the Cabinet remained deadlocked over franchise reform. Many ministers, probably a majority, would have preferred to introduce a bill dealing solely with soldiers' registration. This was blocked by Henderson and Cecil, who insisted that women's suffrage be included in any legislation. At one point they went so far as to imply that they would resign if arrangements were not made to include the addition of women's suffrage to any bill presented to the Commons [89]. This pressure was important in ensuring the government did not proceed during the late summer/early autumn of 1916 with a limited bill which ignored women.

Mrs Pankhurst's intervention threatened to undermine the NUWSS effort to ensure that women's suffrage was included in any franchise bill. At a crucial point in August 1916 when women's suffrage might have been excluded from the legislation, Mrs Pankhurst had it announced in the House of Commons that the WSPU would not insist that women's suffrage be included in a measure to provide the franchise for soldiers and sailors [72]. This undercut the NUWSS effort to link the two together, but fortunately for suffrage advocates it was ignored. Pankhurst's action does, however, help to explain why, when the March 1917 deputation from suffrage societies to the prime minister was being organized, the participants unanimously opposed having Mrs Pankhurst as a member of the deputation [52].

In September 1916 Fawcett observed that public opinion on the suffrage issue had changed remarkably since the war began [53]. Several national newspapers, such as the *Observer*, which had opposed women's suffrage reversed themselves and endorsed it. In July the Liberal Party's Chief Whip, John Gulland, reported privately that there had been a 'very marked' change in public opinion with respect to women's suffrage [87 *p. 140*]. The following month Asquith admitted that if the franchise was extended to all servicemen, as some were proposing, then women would have to be considered.

THE SPEAKER'S CONFERENCE

Unable to reach agreement on the franchise issue, the government established a Speaker's Conference chaired by James Lowther, the Speaker of the House of Commons, to report on the matter. Given the extent of the opposition to women's suffrage, its inclusion in the Speaker's Report was not inevitable. Lowther's selection of the conference participants was crucial to the outcome. Although personally opposed to women's suffrage, Lowther wished to resolve the issue and attempted to select an equal number of reform proponents and opponents from the list of names the government whips provided him. Among those chosen were two of the NUWSS's key parliamentary spokesmen: Willoughby Dickinson and John Simon. The balance of opinion on women's suffrage within the conference was upset by the resignation of four Conservatives who objected that the decisions it was making were too radical. Lowther replaced them with MPs who were sympathetic towards reform. This may have been decisive in enabling the conference to include women's suffrage in its report [89].

While the conference was sitting, Asquith's coalition government was replaced by one with Lloyd George as prime minister. This improved the prospects for women's suffrage since a prime minister who had been the main barrier to reform was replaced by one sympathetic to enfranchising women. But the new government's position remained uncertain because the change resulted in two powerful opponents of women's suffrage being appointed to the Cabinet: Lord Curzon and Lord Milner.

Because women's suffrage was so controversial, the conference delayed considering it until January 1917, after the other issues had been resolved. By a vote of fifteen to six the members indicated support for women's suffrage, but they rejected equal suffrage by a vote of twelve to ten. Dickinson then put forward a proposal to grant the vote to women who were either 'occupiers' themselves or the wives of occupiers. This was adopted by a nine to eight vote. Concerned that women would still be a majority of the electorate, the members then agreed that an age limit should also be imposed, but that it should be left to parliament to decide whether to make it 30 or 35 [89].

Women's suffrage advocates in the conference were concerned that women's organizations might reject the report and initiate a campaign for equal franchise rights. Before the report was published Dickinson informed Fawcett that it would contain something 'very substantial' for women, and urged her to persuade the women's groups to accept it even though it did not provide all that some desired. He warned that if the women's organizations rejected the report's proposals, the government might drop women's suffrage from its scheme [89] [*Doc. 24*].

Although Fawcett had helped shape Dickinson's proposal before it was presented to the Speaker's Conference [*Doc. 25*], this did not guarantee NUWSS acceptance. From its beginning in the 1860s the women's suffrage movement had demanded votes for women on the same terms as men. Since the Speaker's Report did not provide this, one of Fawcett's crucial contributions to reform was in persuading suffragists to accept a measure which some viewed as a defeat. When the NUWSS executive considered the report's proposal for women's suffrage, Rathbone objected that it excluded most of the female factory workers [*Doc. 26*]. But by an eleven to seven vote the executive rejected her request for permission to start a press campaign for alternative proposals for women's suffrage and proceeded to endorse the Speaker's Report with only one dissentient.

Suffragists outside the NUWSS were divided by the Speaker's Report. The National Council for Adult Suffrage objected to women being treated differently from men and to exclusion of most female munitions workers by the age requirement. Some, including Catherine Marshall and Sylvia Pankhurst, proposed to work through the ILP for the removal of the restrictions on women. Margaret Llewelyn Davies indicated she and the Women's Co-operative Guild would continue to fight for adult suffrage [31]. The Manchester and District (Women's Suffrage) Federation initiated a campaign among female munitions workers in the north of England to alter the Speaker's proposals for women [80]. But the possibility of generating pressure within the Labour movement for a wider reform was effectively ended in March 1917 when the Labour Party's special suffrage conference endorsed the Speaker's Report [58].

While inclusion in the Speaker's Report was a major step toward reform, it did not guarantee that women's suffrage would be part of the bill implementing it. This became one of Fawcett's priorities during the crucial period of February-March 1917. She led a deputation from 22 suffrage societies that met with Walter Long, the Local Government Board's President, in February. The deputation pledged that if the government would agree to include the Speaker's Report proposals in its bill then the women's societies would accept them and not agitate for a broader reform – i.e., equal franchise. Long, who had been opposed to women's suffrage, recommended the Cabinet accept this offer on the ground that the proposals were very limited and acceptance would prevent pressure for more radical change [89].

CONSERVATIVE OPPOSITION TO REFORM

The overwhelming vote in favour of the Representation of the People Bill during its second reading has encouraged the belief that only a small group of diehards opposed franchise reform. But this perception of a broad consensus for reform is a myth. Conservative opposition was so strong that the government delayed nearly two months before deciding to proceed with legislation.

Conservatives were divided by the proposed franchise reform. At a meeting of Conservative MPs and peers on 1 March 1917, a large majority opposed introducing legislation based on the Speaker's Report. Shortly after the meeting over 100 Conservative backbenchers, about two-thirds of those present in Westminster, signed a petition to this effect. While this resistance in part reflected an anti-democratic animosity to the extension of the suffrage to more men as well as to women, the 'fiercest' objection came from women's suffrage opponents [118 *p. 904*].

Conservative opponents divided the Cabinet and nearly prevented reform. Long took the initiative in urging the government to act, proposing that the matter be dealt with at the 5 February Cabinet meeting. But immediate action was prevented by opposition from prominent Conservatives, led by Sir George Younger, the party chairman. Curzon led the opposition to women's suffrage within the Cabinet. While Bonar Law and Balfour were prepared to accept women's suffrage, they were reluctant to proceed with legislation if it was controversial.

Asquith's proposal to introduce a House of Commons motion to adopt the Speaker's Report helped break the impasse. Although it was not debated in the House of Commons until 28 March, Lloyd George agreed to Asquith's plan as early as 26 February. It had significant advantages for reform advocates. Legislation could be introduced as a House of Commons bill rather than a government bill; this would enable the Cabinet to proceed without requiring opponents, such as Curzon, to resign from the government.

The Cabinet deadlock was resolved at a tense 26 March meeting. Following Lloyd George's proposal that they proceed with a bill, Sir George Younger and Lord Edmond Talbot, respectively the Conservative Party chairman and the party chief whip, raised strong objections. If all the Conservatives had followed their lead the proposal would likely have been abandoned, but Long and Lord Robert Cecil spoke forcefully for legislation and Bonar Law reluctantly gave his assent. With the Conservatives divided, Henderson's insistence on reform apparently was decisive. Although the Cabinet agreed to proceed with legislation, opponents secured an important concession: the government whips would not be applied to secure passage of the women's suffrage clause and if it was defeated the rest of the bill would not be affected [89].

House of Commons sentiment on franchise reform was tested by the 28 March division. Asquith moved that a House of Commons bill be introduced embodying the Speaker's Conference Report's proposals. Asquith urged that women's suffrage be included in the bill, but he did not do so on the ground that female munitions workers had earned the vote by their contribution to the war effort as is often claimed. Instead, he maintained that when the war ended important issues concerning the future of women in the labour force would have to be resolved, and that women should have the right to express their views through the ballot when reconstruction issues were being decided. Lloyd George and Bonar Law supported Asquith's motion, but Conservative backbenchers were divided. Although the House endorsed Asquith's motion by a vote of 343 to 64, all the opponents were Conservatives, while only 79 Conservatives supported it [89].

SUFFRAGE DEPUTATION

Concerned that the new government might ignore the Speaker's Report, Fawcett had asked Lloyd George to meet a deputation from the suffrage societies on 29 March. Although his statement to the House of Commmons on the previous night had conceded their main concern, the deputation raised several other issues. Remembering the outcome of the 1912 Reform Bill, Fawcett pressed Lloyd George to pledge that women's suffrage would be part of the original bill and not left to be added by amendment. She also requested that the government whips be applied in support of the bill's women's suffrage clause. Others, such as Mary Macarthur, expressed concern that women munition workers who had contributed so much to the war effort would be denied the vote under the Speaker's Report [*Doc. 27*].

Lloyd George's cautious reply to the deputation reflected the struggle still occurring with anti-suffrage forces. While he assured them that a bill would be introduced, and that it would include women's suffrage, he indicated that it would be a House of Commons rather than a government bill. He claimed that because of this he could not say whether the whips would be used for any part of the bill. He also informed them that the government would leave it to the House of Commons to decide whether the voting age for women would be set at 30 or 35.

REPRESENTATION OF THE PEOPLE BILL

On 19 June 1917 the House of Commons voted 385 to 55 to accept the Representation of the People Bill's women's suffrage clause. Suffragists were astonished by the margin of victory. The NUWSS had been uncertain about the outcome because the government whips would not be applied to guarantee passage. To compensate for this, NUWSS members had been urged to contact their MPs, and on the day of the division the NUWSS's unofficial whips were activated to ensure that known supporters did not leave the House of Commons before the vote was taken. The huge majority that ensued was important later in forestalling opposition from the House of Lords.

While it has been assumed that the large majority reflected MPs' appreciation of women's war work, Martin Pugh's analysis of the division suggests that this was primarily a continuation of the pre-1914 parliamentary majority for women's suffrage. Of the 194 MPs who voted in both the 1911 and the 1917 women's suffrage divisions, eighteen changed in favour and four changed against, an increase of only fourteen [92].

If women's suffrage was so bitterly opposed, why did it pass the House of Commons with an overwhelming majority? Conservative resistance declined dramatically after March for a variety of reasons. Many of the Conservative MPs who voted for the bill were anti-suffragists who changed sides rather than opinions. Some shared Long's view that reform was inevitable, and that conceding a limited measure of reform now would postpone more radical change (such as equal franchise) for 20 to 30 years. Other anti-suffragists refrained from voting against the bill because they feared retribution by female voters if the measure passed [130]. Also, by the time the vote was taken, MPs had become aware that Conservative opinion in the constituencies favoured reform; 98 constituency parties supported women's suffrage, while 44 opposed it [96].

The overwhelming vote for women's suffrage also reflected the fact that it was an extremely conservative measure. Despite wartime publicity about the nation's gratitude to female munitions workers, the 1918 legislation left most of them disenfranchised because they were under 30. Women over 30 were believed to be less likely to support feminist or radical reforms than those who were younger. Also, women who had reached age 30 were more likely to be married and to be mothers, factors which were expected to make them less susceptible to radical class or gender movements [72]. Finally, the educated women who had been an important source of support for the suffrage movement and who flocked into white-collar employment in the 1920s, often remained voteless. Because they typically rented furnished lodgings or lived with their parents, they did not qualify as local government electors and thus did not gain the parliamentary franchise; many female teachers found themselves excluded for this reason [11].

Although the women's societies had pledged not to attempt to amend the bill's proposal for parliamentary suffrage, they did not sit passively while it was passing through the House of Commons. When it was discovered that many of the women to be enfranchised would still be excluded from voting in local government elections, the NUWSS initiated a campaign under Rathbone's direction to alter the bill to extend the local government franchise to them as well [106]. At first the government refused to accept the NUWSS proposal and applied the whips to prevent it from gaining support. But the NUWSS orchestrated such a flood of letters and telegrams to ministers that the government withdrew the whips, and on a free vote the House of Commons included the NUWSS-sponsored clause in the bill [28].

Fawcett had anticipated the House of Lords would be a formidable obstacle. Anti-suffrage sentiment was strong there and peers did not have to face re-election. Lord Curzon, President of the National League for Opposing Woman Suffrage, was expected to lead the resistance in the Lords. But after enumerating the reasons why women's suffrage was inappropriate, Curzon announced that in order to avoid a clash between the Lords and the Commons he would not oppose the bill. This seemed to dishearten others who were considering voting against the measure, and the Lords then voted for it, 134 to 71 [130].

The 1918 Representation of the People Act granted the vote to 8,400,000 women, who comprised 39.6 per cent of the electorate. The Act is often mistakenly said to have enfranchised women aged 30 and above. In addition to the age requirement, it restricted the vote to those women who were also local government electors or the wives of local government electors. It is estimated that about 22 per cent of the women aged 30 or above were excluded from voting by this additional requirement; many of these were working-class or unmarried employed women [109]. If it is understood that the women enfranchised by the 1918 Act were disproportionately middle-class housewives aged 30 and above, then the tendency of women to vote Conservative in the 1920s becomes less surprising [111].

Fawcett considered the enactment of the suffrage legislation the greatest moment in her life. Suffrage societies sponsored a victory party at the Queen's Hall in March 1918 for which William Blake's poem, 'Jerusalem', was set to music as the suffrage hymn. But suffragist celebrations were muted by their awareness that they had not obtained the equal suffrage rights for which they had been campaigning since the 1860s. Since the Act gave the vote to men at nineteen if they had seen active service in the armed forces (and to all men at age twenty-one), it preserved women's different and inferior status under the law [130]. While few went as far as Dora Montefiore in accusing the suffrage societies of having 'betrayed' their supporters by accepting legislation that fell short of equality, reformers were aware that they had won a battle, not the war [20 *p. 194*].

6 EQUAL FRANCHISE, 1919–1928

Historians have virtually ignored the post-1918 equal franchise campaign. Sylvia Pankhurst claimed that the 1928 Representation of the People Act came 'virtually without effort' [22 *p. 608*]; her assumption that it was inevitable, and accomplished with little struggle, has been widely accepted. The fact that women's organizations tended to be less visible and played a less dramatic role than in the prewar campaign may explain why women's historians have neglected it. This chapter suggests that these assumptions need rethinking: equal franchise was obtained only after an intense decade-long struggle in which women were active participants.

Certainly there was nothing inevitable about the Conservative Party introducing equal franchise reform, especially by lowering it to age 21. During the 1920s the party was divided by that issue. Although Conservative Party leaders consistently expressed support for the principle, Conservative MPs provided 84 per cent of the opponents in the suffrage divisions in 1919, 1920 and 1924; in the 1919 and 1924 divisions more Conservatives voted against reform than voted for it [53]. The struggle over the 1928 Representation of the People Bill was primarily between the Conservative Government and its back-benchers; the other two parties supported it. Since even Conservatives who wanted equal franchise reform generally preferred that it be granted at age 25, the fact that a Conservative government reduced women's voting age to 21 requires explanation.

The case for equal franchise did not rest solely on the inequity in sex differentiated voting ages. Although employed women might be regarded as a group particularly in need of the vote, the 1918 Act ensured that women who worked for pay were especially likely to be voteless. In the 1920s it was estimated that only about one of every fifteen employed women had the vote. Women working in industry were typically young and unmarried and thus disqualified by the age limit. But many professional women, even those over age 30, were ineligible to vote. Because many professions had a marriage bar, most were single and unable to qualify through their husbands' eligibility. Moreover, since most professional women rented furnished accommodations, they did not meet the property qualification. It is not known whether the 1918 Act was intended to have this consequence, but it kept most of the educated women who worked for a living disenfranchised, even though they presumably would have been particularly well-informed voters [15] [*Doc. 28*].

During the 1920s there were three main sources of organized pressure for equal franchise: feminist societies, the Conservative Party women's organization and Labour Party women. After the principle of women's suffrage was conceded in 1918, the NUWSS reformed itself as the National Union of Societies for Equal Citizenship* (NUSEC). Eleanor Rathbone replaced Millicent Fawcett as president in 1919. The NUSEC adopted a new programme that included equal franchise at age 21. Several prewar societies joined with it in the suffrage campaign: the Women's Freedom League, the London Society for Women's Service* (previously the London Society for Women's Suffrage), and St Joan's Social and Political Alliance (previously the Catholic Women's Suffrage Society). These were reinforced by two new groups: Lady Rhondda formed the Six Point Group in February 1921 to work for gender equality (although it did not add equal franchise to its 'Immediate Programme' until 1926) and in March 1921 Lady Astor established the Consultative Committee of Women's Organizations to co-ordinate efforts by women's groups to pressure parliament for legislation to improve women's status [104].

The 1918 Representation of the People Act enfranchised an additional five million men, most of them working class and expected to become Labour voters. Confronted with the problem of how to widen its pool of supporters to offset Labour's gain, the Conservative Party turned to the new female electorate during the 1920s [123]. The first step was the creation of a Conservative women's organization. In 1918 women were allowed to become party members, the Women's Unionist Organisation was established, a Women's Advisory Committee formed, and one-third of the seats on the National Union's Central Council and other party bodies were reserved for women [92].

As it became apparent that women would gain the parliamentary vote, the Labour Party made several changes intended to appeal to the new female electorate. The party's National Executive Committee (NEC) arranged a merger with the Women's Labour League, allowed individual women to join local constituency parties, guaranteed women four seats on the party's executive committee, and recognized the Standing Joint Committee of Industrial Women's Organizations (SJCIWO) as the party's women's advisory committee. At the 1918 party conference Arthur Henderson welcomed the new female voters into the Labour Party as 'equal partners'. In its 1918 general election manifesto the party pledged support for the immediate extension of the vote to women at age 21.

In 1919 the Labour Party introduced the Women's Emancipation Bill that would have allowed women to vote at 21. The bill temporarily brought feminist and Labour women's organizations into alliance. While it was under consideration by parliament, the NUSEC and the SJCIWO sent a joint deputation to the home secretary urging the government to support the bill, and later joined forces in sponsoring a public rally to arouse support for the measure [137].

Although the Coalition government's 1918 election manifesto pledged that it would 'remove all existing inequalities of the law as between men and women' [36 *p. 16*], it reacted with alarm to the progress of the Women's Emancipation Bill through the House of Commons. The government applied the whips in an attempt to defeat the bill, but despite this the House of Commmons passed it on its second reading by a vote of 100 to 88. Coalition MPs braved the whips' displeasure because for a brief period in 1919 they were even more fearful of the newly enfranchised voters. Women's groups had made clear the high priority they gave to the bill's enactment, and MPs anticipated that women would vote as a gender bloc to defeat those who opposed it [104].

Equal franchise bills were introduced almost every year in the early 1920s, but despite strong parliamentary support most were blocked by government opposition. In 1920 a NUSEC-backed Labour Party bill passed its second reading in the House of Commons with a large majority, but the government killed it during the committee stage. In 1921 NUSEC obtained the signatures of almost 200 MPs to an equal franchise memorial which was presented to the prime minister. In the following year NUSEC lobbied intensively for Lord Robert Cecil's Women's Enfranchisement Bill which passed its second reading in the House of Commons by a 208 to 60 vote, but the government fell from office before it could become law. In 1923 the NUSEC secured the signatures of over 200 MPs to an equal franchise memorial presented in conjunction with Isaac Foot's Women's Enfranchisement Bill but it was also unsuccessful.

THE LABOUR GOVERNMENT AND FRANCHISE REFORM

Since the Labour Party had consistently advocated equal franchise, and had stated in its 1923 election manifesto that it stood for 'equal political and legal rights', reformers expected the 1924 Labour government to introduce suffrage legislation. Although the government did agree to make William Adamson's private member's equal franchise bill a government measure after it reached the committee stage, it did not allow parliamentary time for it to proceed through its later stages before the government resigned.

Feminists felt betrayed by the Labour government's reluctance to sponsor reform and publicly criticized it. Although Rathbone had sought closer ties between feminists and Labour women, she reported to the NUSEC Annual Council meeting that Labour had broken faith with the women who had supported it: 'Has a party in office no responsibility towards its principles and past professions and pledges?' [31 *p. 145*].

Although equal franchise provided a basis for a united women's movement in the 1920s, class and party affiliation provided competing identities that hampered efforts to develop gender solidarity. The Labour Party considered feminist groups to be rivals for women's allegiance and feared that they would encourage a gender consciousness that would undercut Labour's class-based ideology. At the 1918 and 1920 Labour Party women's conferences resolutions were passed urging Labour women not to join single-sex (feminist) organizations as 'they would be in danger of getting their political opinions muddled' [137 *p. 24*]. The SJCIWO refused to join Astor's Consultative Committee in 1921 because of this resolution [137].

The General Strike heightened class feeling which further undermined links between the feminist movement and the Labour Party. The Labour Party NEC intervened to stop the SJCIWO from co-operating with feminist groups campaigning for equal franchise even though the SJCIWO (and the Labour Party) continued to support that reform. Although the SJCIWO had been participating in NUSEC sponsored activities, early in 1927 Labour's NEC denied it permission to send representatives to a suffrage rally, claiming that the NUSEC 'industrial and social policy was not sound' [137 *p. 33*]. Later that year the SJCIWO notified the NUSEC it would no longer be able to co-operate in the suffrage campaign or other matters so long as the NUSEC continued its opposition to protective legislation for women.

Strong party ties hampered efforts by the women's societies to pressure political parties on the suffrage issue. At the October 1924

Consultative Committee of Women's Organisations meeting, Eva Hubback, the NUSEC representative, admitted that the Labour Party had not mentioned equal suffrage in its election manifesto. But because the party was sympathetic to reform she urged the committee not to express its indignation but to simply send it a resolution urging it to support women's suffrage. When a resolution was proposed expressing regret that the Conservative government was only committed to holding a conference on the subject, which could lead to reform being postponed indefinitely, the committee divided. Some thought the resolution unfairly critical of the Conservative Party; others did not think it strong enough. Eventually the resolution was withdrawn, and one expressing dissatisfaction with all three party manifestos was passed [1].

By the mid-1920s the problem suffrage reformers had to overcome was not overt opposition to equal franchise. Labour and Conservative Party leaders repeatedly expressed support for the principle of equal franchise, and few politicians publicly opposed it. But endorsing the principle had become a substitute for action; political leaders coupled their approval of equal franchise with claims that the time was not yet right to introduce it. The difficulty for reformers was how to move politicians from a general acceptance of the principle to a commitment to implement it.

WOMEN AND THE CONSERVATIVE PARTY

Reformers benefited from Conservative Party leaders' awareness that women had become vital to the party's future [123]. In the 1920s the women's organisation was the party's most rapidly growing unit. By 1924 there were women's branches in 355 constituencies; by 1928 paid female party membership had grown to nearly one million. Conservative Party professionals acknowledged that the house-to-house membership recruiting and canvassing by Conservative Party women made an important contribution to the October 1924 general election victory [134]. The party also became increasingly dependent on the women's organization for fundraising. By the end of the 1920s the women's branches were raising the greater proportion of the money used to finance Conservative constituency associations.

Women voters were also crucial to the Conservative Party's electoral success in the 1920s. During that decade women were more likely than men to vote Conservative; the higher the proportion of women in a constituency, the less well the Labour candidate tended to do [134]. Conservative voting in the 1924 general election tended to rise in proportion to the number of female voters in the constituency; in those constituencies where women comprised more than 40 per cent of the electorate, Conservative candidates gained more than 48 per cent of the total vote [92].

Conservative Party leaders were stunned by the party's defeat in the 1923 general election. They believed the loss of support from female voters was a key factor. Sir George Younger, the party chairman, claimed women had voted against them out of fear that its recently announced support for tariffs would make food more expensive [92]. It is understandable, then, that the party should have made special efforts to attract female voters in the 1924 general election.

CONSERVATIVE PARTY REFORM PLEDGE

Although the 1924 Conservative Party election manifesto made greater efforts to appeal to women, it contained no reference to women's suffrage. But just before the election Stanley Baldwin, the party leader, declared that the Conservative Party supported equal political rights for women. He made no commitment as to how soon it might implement this pledge. He did, however, indicate that if the party was returned to office it would propose an all-party conference on franchise reform similar to the 1916 Speaker's Conference.

Suffrage advocates were uncertain as to how firmly Baldwin had committed a Conservative government to reform. Those who were not Conservatives suspected that Baldwin's statement was intended to attract female voters while leaving a Conservative government free to postpone action into the indefinite future. Some prominent Conservatives, including Winston Churchill, privately believed Baldwin had merely pledged support for the equal franchise principle without making any commitment to act beyond sponsoring a conference.

Baldwin's proposal to hold an all-party conference was politically shrewd. It enabled suffrage reformers to believe he was proceeding toward reform, while allowing opponents to view it as a means of blocking it. In addition to holding his party together, Baldwin apparently also hoped that through it he could commit the Labour Party to an agreed measure granting equal franchise at age 25 [36, 11]. This would have permitted him to fulfil his equal franchise pledge while gaining approval from anti-democratic Conservatives who wished to minimize the increase in the electorate. But, if this was his plan, it collapsed when Labour refused to agree to setting the voting age at 25 [118, 36].

How the 1924 Conservative government came to introduce equal franchise at age 21 has been a matter of controversy. The Cabinet faced three main issues. Should it limit itself to proposing an all-party conference without any commitment to action if the conference was deadlocked? Should it agree to introduce franchise legislation in the current parliament? If equal franchise was to be introduced, should it be granted at age 21 or 25?

The conflicting views as to what the government's policy was stemmed from the ambiguity of Baldwin's declaration on franchise reform. In pledging the party to equal political rights during the 1924 election campaign, Baldwin stated that the question should be settled, 'if possible', by agreement, and that an all-party conference be appointed to accomplish this. This, of course, left open the question of what the Conservative government would do if it was not possible to settle the matter by agreement. The statement may have been deliberately vague because the party was so divided on the issue. It was interpreted by reformers as indicating a preference to proceed with reform via the method of an all-party conference, but it implied a commitment to introduce equal franchise regardless of whether this method was used. Reform opponents interpreted it as supporting the equal franchise principle but without any commitment to action other than sponsoring a conference which might be unable to reach agreement.

The introduction of a private member's equal franchise bill in February 1925 forced the Cabinet to consider its position. The minutes indicate the Cabinet agreed that Sir William Joynson Hicks, the Home Secretary, was to announce the government's opposition to the bill. In doing so, he was to refer to the prime minister's 1924 election pledge and to state that the government intended to give effect to it later in the present parliament by proposing an all-party conference. When he addressed the House of Commons, Joynson Hicks stated that the government was committed to equal franchise before the next general election. The House then voted for a government amendment proposing that 'a considered scheme of franchise reform' should be introduced into the House 'within the lifetime of the present Parliament' [36 *p. 25*].

Churchill later claimed that by his statement Joynson Hicks had inadvertently pledged the government to introduce equal franchise before the end of the current parliament without Cabinet authorization. But Baldwin, who surely knew what his pledge meant, was sitting next to Joynson Hicks when the latter spoke and made no objection. Furthermore, when Baldwin spoke later in the debate he did not repudiate Joynson Hicks's statement. Joynson Hicks responded to

Churchill's claim by pointing out that the Cabinet had approved the amendment put to the House, and in doing so had agreed to franchise reform in the current parliament, with or without a conference. Churchill's insistence that the Cabinet had only approved a scheme of franchise reform that emerged from an all-party conference may have stemmed from his hope that the latter would be deadlocked, thus preventing reform.

WOMEN'S REFORM STRATEGIES

By the mid-1920s the lack of visible progress towards reform had begun to produce tension between the women's societies. Rathbone, Rhondda, and Astor urged three alternative strategies to improve this situation. Under Rathbone's leadership the NUSEC continued its quiet non-partisan lobbying of the three major parties. Impatient with the NUSEC's lack of success, Lady Rhondda sought to invigorate the suffrage campaign. She intended to bring Mrs Pankhurst into it, and to revive the suffragette tactic of protest demonstrations. In 1926, Rhondda established the Equal Political Rights Demonstration Committee* as a step in this direction. Its original purpose was solely to organize the Hyde Park mass meeting on 3 July which was supported by 40 women's groups. Nearly 3,000 women participated in the first suffrage procession since the First World War; the press portrayed it as a revival of the spirit of prewar militancy.

But after the rally the EPRDC was reorganized as the Equal Political Rights Campaign Committee with continuing responsibility for gingering up the suffrage campaign. Although the Six Point Group, the WFL, St Joan's and the National Union of Women Teachers supported this step, it was opposed by the NUSEC, the LNSWS and the National Council of Women. NUSEC leaders recognized that the change was an attempt to wrest control of the suffrage campaign out of their hands and feared the ex-suffragette Rhondda would resurrect militant tactics that would prevent reform.

Rhondda thought it important for women to take an active and visible role in pressuring the government to grant equal suffrage so that they could be seen to have been responsible for reform. Lady Astor, among others, warned her against this. Astor was orchestrating pressure from Conservative women within the party structure and was convinced that Baldwin would proceed with reform unless a revival of suffragette militancy occurred [54].

Uncertainty about the government's position contributed to tensions within the women's groups as to what they should demand. At the Consultative Committee's October 1926 meeting the societies disagreed over how they should respond if the government did proceed to set up a franchise conference. Hubback, speaking for the NUSEC, thought they should accept, but withdrew her suggestion when the WFL and St Joan's representatives opposed it on the ground that it was just a ploy to avoid introducing legislation [1].

Feminists were also divided as to whether they should accept if the government proposed equal franchise at age 25 or hold out for age 21. Although the NUSEC was pledged to fight for age 21, in November 1925 it urged the Consultative Committee to accept age 25; this was opposed by the WFL and St. Joan's representatives [1]. Lady Astor also urged the women's organizations to accept age 25 if the government offered it. Rathbone privately agreed on the necessity of compromise but feared that Lady Rhondda would not accept it. If the government proposed suffrage at age 25 Rathbone planned to 'get on her [Rhondda] at once . . . and try to make her take the same line' [31 *p. 187*].

Astor's efforts to mobilize Conservative Party women to pressure the government were hampered by the divisions within their ranks. The 1926 Conservative Party women's conference defeated a motion calling for equal franchise at age 21 but passed one urging that it be granted at age 25. When the party's Women's Advisory Committee discussed the issue on 16 November 1926 they found that Conservative women were divided between those who wished: (1) that women be given the vote at age 21; (2) that equal franchise be granted at age 25; and (3) that reform be limited to removing the anomalies in the current law so that all women aged 30 and above could vote. They were in agreement, however, that the government had made a promise to deal with the issue, and that it would be 'disastrous' if it did not do so before the next election. A memorandum summarizing their position was forwarded to the home secretary [*Doc. 29*].

On the following day the Cabinet agreed to create an equal franchise subcommittee to recommend how to implement the government's pledge to secure equal political rights for women. The subcommittee quickly agreed that an all-party conference was not desirable as it would simply enable the Labour Party to champion votes for women at age 21. J. C. C. Davidson, the Conservative Party Chairman, and the Conservative Central Office both warned the subcommittee that equal franchise at age 21 would be detrimental to party interests. Davidson stated that it was politically impracticable to maintain the franchise age for women at age 30, and thus he and Central Office recommended that equal franchise at age 25 would be the most satisfactory solution from the party's point of view [*Doc. 30*]. Perhaps because of the strong feeling developing within the subcommittee in support of this policy, after three meetings Baldwin and Joynson Hicks announced that discussion would be continued in the Cabinet and the subcommittee was terminated.

The Cabinet was divided into two roughly equal factions by the franchise issue. Churchill and Lord Birkenhead (F. E. Smith) vehemently opposed equal franchise at twenty-one. Churchill may have been one of the ministers who made vague resignation threats in an attempt to block reform; he felt so strongly that he insisted that his name be recorded as opposing the Cabinet's decision and attached a memorandum of dissent to the Cabinet conclusion. But Joynson Hicks, Lord Eustace Percy and Lord Robert Cecil insisted that the government was committed to proceeding with reform. They noted that the party chairman and the Conservative Central Office were now recommending granting equal franchise at age 21 on the ground that if they didn't the next Labour government certainly would, thereby obtaining the political loyalty of the female voters. Although most of the Cabinet would have preferred equal franchise at age 25, the majority reluctantly accepted that this was politically impossible, and on 12 April 1927 agreed to grant votes to women at age 21 [118] [*Doc. 31*].

Although this ended Cabinet discussion, opponents waged a last-ditch effort during 1927 to arouse Conservative Party opinion against equal franchise at age 21. The *Daily Mail* published a series of misleading articles claiming that the proposed reform meant giving the vote to 'flappers'. By portraying the latter as young, unmarried, independent, sexually active and ignorant of politics, the *Daily Mail* constructed a mixture of negative gender and generational stereotypes calculated to stir Conservative opinion against reform [84]. Even after the Cabinet decision, in apparent violation of the principle of collective responsibility, Birkenhead continued to publish articles opposing equal franchise at age 21. It was because they believed some Cabinet ministers were organising a campaign to shelve the proposed equal franchise legislation that the Equal Political Rights Campaign Committee's leaders decided to go ahead with the suffrage demonstration planned for 16 July.

Equal franchise legislation would make women a majority of the electorate and much of the opposition to it reflected fears that women would use the vote to introduce gender-related changes. Some objected to the reform on the ground that it would mean men would be ruled by women. Others expressed concern that women would vote as a gender bloc, bringing about the fundamental transformation of male political culture that many suffragists desired. Suffrage leaders focused on this point when they sought to allay resistance in the House of Lords prior to its vote on the Representation of the People Bill [31]. Underlying much of this resistance was the concern that the younger women who would be enfranchised were more likely to be single and therefore more inclined to be feminist than older or married women [*Doc. 32*].

Equal suffrage advocates devoted much of their efforts to reassuring opponents that the political divisions among women were as great as those dividing men. But they also stressed that the women enfranchised under the 1918 Act were primarily married women, mostly homemakers, and that their interests were not identical to those of single women, many of whom were employed. This meant that when legislation affecting employed women was considered in parliament, MPs did not have to be concerned about the views of the women whose interests would be affected. Feminists focused on this unfair exclusion of employed women in letters to *The Times* and in their 8 March 1927 deputation to the prime minister [*Doc. 33*].

The Conservative Party became reconciled to equal franchise legislation in the course of an intense intraparty debate in 1927. At the beginning of that year the majority of Conservatives appear to have been divided between those wanting no action other than holding an all-party conference and those desiring equal franchise at age 25. By the end of 1927 the party had not only accepted equal franchise, but at age 21. Political expediency may have contributed more to this change than conversion to the principle of gender equality. A majority of Central Office Agents had concluded by March that equal franchise at age 25 was impractical; it would antagonize large numbers of men while not satisfying the women who desired equal franchise at 21. Furthermore, the next Labour government would almost certainly lower the voting age to 21 which would result in the newly enfranchised women becoming Labour voters. But a majority of the constituency associations which had expressed their view to the National Union executive by June 1927 favoured equal franchise at age 25. Given the continuing division within the party, the position taken by the annual party conference was of considerable importance. Although three resolutions were submitted opposing equal franchise at age 21, the conference endorsed the resolution favoring equal franchise at age 21 submitted by a member of the Conservative Party Central Council.

Although the Representation of the People (Equal Franchise) Bill passed its second reading in the House of Commons in March 1928 by the overwhelming vote of 387 to 10, this does not accurately reflect the size and intensity of the opposition. The huge majority reflected prudence on the part of MPs who realized the bill was going to pass and that the female electorate could determine their political future. Although a few Conservative diehards spoke against the bill during the debate, the real struggle had already occurred before the measure reached the House of Commons.

As a result of the Act, women became a majority of the electorate, comprising 52.7 per cent of the potential voters. The attacks on the 'flapper vote' by equal franchise opponents obscured the fact that the Act enfranchised more women over 30 than under 25. Of the additional 5.5 million women who gained the vote, 1,950,000 were over age 30, while 1,590,000 were under age 25 [15].

Although the 1928 Act was the culmination of a 61-year campaign for equal voting rights, reformers had mixed feelings. Some, like Lady Rhondda, thought it a 'blessed relief' that the matter was over so that they could drop the reforming business and get on with other aspects of life [31]. Reflecting on the anti-feminist reaction in the 1920s that, among other setbacks, had recently resulted in some London hospitals refusing to admit female medical students, Vera Brittain doubted that the struggle was really over. Aware that the suffrage campaign had originated amidst expectations that women's suffrage would bring about a transformation of society, Brittain asked whether equal franchise meant women had 'really rounded seraglio point' [48 *p. 182*], or whether it had been granted because male politicians no longer feared women would vote as a bloc for gender reforms. If women were simply drawn into the existing parties and lacked the power to shape party programmes to protect their interests, Britain anticipated that equal franchise would have little effect on existing gender structures [48]. If this should prove to be the case, equal franchise should be viewed as one stage of a continuing campaign to eliminate discrimination against women rather than a final victory.

PART TWO: ASSESSMENT

The women's suffrage movement was a watershed in British women's history. It brought women together in a mass movement unparalleled in British history. It was successful in gaining equal voting rights for women, the right of women to be elected to parliament, and contributed to the admission of women to the political parties. But for participants the sense of accomplishment was diluted by the awareness that the larger goal of undermining gender structures had eluded them.

Earlier studies viewed the suffrage campaign as narrowly concerned with equal political rights, and as a continuation of the movement towards political democracy associated with the Reform Acts of 1832, 1867, and 1884. It is now considered part of the gender reform movement initiated by Victorian feminists that was directed against women's subordinate roles in education, employment and the family, as well as in politics. It was, in short, a movement for women's emancipation, rather than just for female enfranchisement.

The changed interpretation of the suffrage campaign in part stems from new understandings of its ideological basis. While some suffragists based their claim on an equal rights ideology rooted in liberal political theory, recent work has stressed the importance of a sexual difference ideology which maintained that women's natures were different from men's and superior in important respects [38, 76]. This encouraged the perception that the vote would do more than simply allow women to vote as men did; it would empower women to alter man-made institutions to reflect women's higher moral standards. This was especially evident with respect to the double standard of sexuality, but it underlay a variety of other issues as well, including the use of force in domestic or international politics. Part of the male anti-suffragist's resistance to enfranchising females stemmed from the fear that women would use political power to feminize social institutions.

Female anti-suffragists have often been ignored or dismissed as suffering from false consciousness. Jane Lewis has rescued them from oblivion by pointing out that the 'vast majority' of female suffragists and anti-suffragists drew upon a shared sexual difference ideology in reaching opposing conclusions about women's suffrage [79 *p. 7*]. Their belief that women's natures were different from men's led female anti-suffragists to argue that women were better suited to local government work in which issues that were part of women's expertise – health, education, and welfare – loomed larger than in national government. They also believed that women benefited from maintaining gender boundaries; they resented the undermining of those boundaries by WSPU militancy because they anticipated it would unleash male violence towards women.

During the Edwardian period the suffrage campaign became a mass movement uniting women in a demand for gender reform fuelled by a consciousness of oppression based on sex. But even during the peak period of gender consciousness competing allegiances divided reformers. Jill Liddington [81] has explored the movement's class dimensions, while Angela John [41, 124] and Leah Leneman [75] have demonstrated the continued importance of national identity. Party ties also threatened to undermine gender unity; Claire Hirshfield has described the anguish of Liberal Party women forced to choose between gender and party loyalties [121]. In the postwar decade class and ideological differences frustrated efforts to re-establish a united women's movement [104, 137].

The relative importance of the NUWSS and the WSPU in gaining the vote continues to be a matter of debate. There is general agreement that the WSPU's militant tactics revitalized the suffrage movement between 1905 and 1908. But the new forms of violence used by the WSPU after 1910 impeded further progress towards franchise reform. Studies by Sandra Holton [58, 61] and Jo Vellacott [112] have suggested that the NUWSS's electoral alliance with the Labour Party was the key development in bringing about women's suffrage.

Antoinette Burton has drawn attention to the danger of viewing the suffrage movement in isolation from the political and cultural context in which it developed. While suffragists sought to establish a 'global sisterhood' through such organizations as the International Woman Suffrage Alliance, they also collaborated in the ideological work of sustaining the British Empire [35]. The tension between these positions was reflected in suffragists' arguments for enfranchisement. Some held that women's suffrage was desirable in order that a masculine political culture relying upon physical force should be replaced by a female culture based upon moral principles. But others believed that women needed the vote in order to help Britain continue to be a great imperial nation. The First World War brought the conflict between the two positions into the open, resulting in the split in the NUWSS in 1915.

When John Stuart Mill proposed in 1866 that women be granted the parliamentary vote, some MPs considered the idea so ludicrous that they laughed. But by 1929 women had equal voting rights with men, women MPs sat in parliament, and all parties were careful to seem attentive to female voters' concerns. This transformation in formal political rights seemed particularly dangerous to some contemporaries because it appeared to give women the power to alter gender structures.

But equal franchise did not bring radical change. Suffrage advocates who believed 'party Government' would disappear and politics would be based upon principles rather than party interests underestimated the forces for continuity [53]. NUSEC membership declined rapidly after 1928, few women were elected MPs, and few reforms were introduced in the following decade that could be clearly identified as resulting from the increase in female voters. This is not to suggest that the women's movement disappeared after 1928; suffragists such as Ray Strachey and Eleanor Rathbone were prominent in the campaigns for equal pay and family allowances in the 1930s and 1940s. The enfranchisement of women made them a potentially powerful political force, especially in close elections. This was an important consideration in the granting of equal pay to female civil servants in the mid-1950s [136]. The growing awareness of the difficulty of using political action to bring about gender reform has been a sobering discovery for many reformers but, if the pace of change has sometimes seemed glacial, change has occurred.

PART THREE: DOCUMENTS

DOCUMENT 1   THE FIRST SUFFRAGE PETITION

In the 1860s the idea of women voting seemed so radical that reformers thought it best to base their proposal on property ownership rather than sex discrimination.

It seems to me that while a Reform Bill is under discussion and petitions are being presented to Parliament from various classes ... it is very desirable that women who wish for political enfranchisement should say so .... I think the most important thing is to make a demand and commence the first humble beginnings of an agitation for which reasons can be given that are in harmony with the political ideas of English people in general. No idea is so universally accepted and acceptable in England as that taxation and representation ought to go together, and people in general will be much more willing to listen to the assertion that single women and widows of property have been unjustly overlooked, and left out from the privileges to which their property entitles them, than to the much more startling general proposition that sex is not a proper ground of distinction in political rights.

It seems to me, therefore, that a petition asking for the admission to the franchise of all women holding the requisite property qualification would be highly desirable now ... .

Helen Taylor to Barbara Bodichon, 9 May, 1866. The Fawcett Library, London Guildhall University, McCrimmon Bodichon Collection.

DOCUMENT 2   SEXUAL DIFFERENCE AND WOMEN'S SUFFRAGE

Although some reformers did base their claim on liberal equal rights ideology, many insisted it was because women were different from men that they should have the right to vote.

With regard to the differences between men and women, those who advocate the enfranchisement of women have no wish to disregard them or make little of them. On the contrary, we base our claim to representation to a large extent on them. If men and women were exactly alike, the representation of men would represent us; but not being alike, that wherein we differ is unrepresented under the present system ... .

But this difference between men and women, instead of being a reason against their enfranchisement, seems to me the strongest possible reason in favour of it; we want the home and the domestic side of things to count for more in politics and in the administration of public affairs than they do at present. We want to know how various kinds of legislative enactments bear on the home and on domestic life. And we want to force our legislators to consider the domestic as well as the political results of any legislation which many of them are advocating ... .

I advocate the extension of the franchise to women because I wish to strengthen true womanliness in woman, and because I want to see the womanly and domestic side of things weigh more and count for more in all public concerns.

Millicent Garrett Fawcett, 'Home and Politics', in Lewis [7], pp. 419, 423.

DOCUMENT 3   THE CASE FOR WOMEN'S SUFFRAGE

Anti-suffragists relied heavily on the idea of separate spheres, with its belief that political life is part of men's sphere because it is based on physical force.

You are generally told that women are not fit to vote ... [but] women are held fit to possess property, and the possession of property is the only fitness for the vote. But if we press for particulars, we are met by the great Nature-argument; we are told of the peculiarities of our nature ... that is, in other words, our physical and mental inferiority ... .

There is one more argument that I must notice – that the basis of government is physical force ... and therefore women being physically the weaker are unfitted for the franchise ... But what is meant by physical force being the basis of government? I have always thought that government was designed to supersede physical force, that civilization meant the reign of law instead of brute-strength ... . Doubtless, before communities were formed, the man who could knock the other down would have most power. But ... our Cabinet ministers are not chosen from the men who can knock each other down.

Arabella Shore, speech delivered to the London National Society for Women's Suffrage in Hollis [6], pp. 309, 311.

DOCUMENT 4   WOMEN AGAINST WOMEN'S SUFFRAGE

Female anti-suffragists were convinced that women's suffrage would erode the difference between men's and women's natures by lowering women to the men's level.

We, the undersigned, wish to appeal to the common sense and the educated thought of the men and women of England against the proposed extension of the Parliamentary suffrage to women.

1. While desiring the fullest possible development of the powers, energies, and education of women, we believe that their work for the State, and their responsibilities towards it, must always differ essentially from those of men ... . To men belong the struggle of debate and legislation in Parliament; the hard and exhausting labour implied in the administration of the national resources and powers; the conduct of England's relations towards the external world; the working of the army and navy ... . In all these spheres women's direct participation is made impossible either by the disabilities of sex, or by strong formations of custom and habit resting ultimately upon physical difference, against which it is useless to contend ... . Therefore, it is not just to give women direct power of deciding questions of Parliamentary policy, of war, of foreign or colonial affairs, of commerce and finance equal to that possessed by men ... .

To sum up: we would give them [women] their full share ... in that higher State which rests on thought, conscience, and moral influence; but we protest against their admission to direct power in that State which does rest upon force – the State in its administrative, military and financial aspects – where the physical capacity ... of men ought to prevail ... .

'An Appeal Against Female Suffrage', *The Nineteenth Century* (June 1889) in Hollis [6], pp. 322–3.

DOCUMENT 5   FAWCETT'S RESPONSE TO FEMALE
              ANTI-SUFFRAGISTS

Millicent Fawcett considered it illogical that voting should be considered a threat to women's femininity but that working for male candidates in parliamentary elections was considered acceptable.

A large part of the Protest [against women's suffrage] is directed against women taking an active part in the turmoil of political life ... . On the other hand, women do not vote in Parliamentary elections, but they are invited and pressed by all parties to take an active part in the turmoil of political life. Among other inconsistencies of the protesting ladies, it should not be forgotten that ... if women are fit to advise, convince, and persuade voters how to vote, they are surely also fit to vote themselves ... .

The 'party nothing but party' politician in England ... looks with distrust on women's suffrage. Women would be an unknown quantity, less amenable to party discipline ... . These fears tell against us very heavily, and we cannot allay them; because the fear that women will be independent and will dare to vote for what they think is right, whether the professional politician likes it or not, is, in our minds, not a fear, but a hope, and a hope which is at the root of all we are working for ... .

We do not want women to be bad imitations of men; we neither deny nor minimise the differences between men and women. The claim of women to representation depends to a large extent on those differences.

Millicent Garrett Fawcett, 'Female Suffrage: A Reply', *The Nineteenth Century* (July 1889) in Hollis [6], pp. 330–1.

DOCUMENT 6   WORKING FOR SUFFRAGE IN THE 1890S

In her autobiography Dora Montefiore conveyed the sense of hopelessness experienced by some suffragists in the 1890s.

I worked for some time [in the 1890s] with the old Suffrage Society under the Presidency of Mrs. Fawcett ... . I was on the Executive Committee, but found it depressing work as the Press would give us no publicity and though we worked hard and conscientiously during twelve months of each year to get the support of Members of Parliament and the public to our hardy annual of a "Bill for the enfranchisement of some women," we found that when the day came round for the Bill to be introduced, it was either talked out or laughed out and that we had to begin once more another year of ... getting up public meetings, unreported by the Press, and of supporting and helping to get elected Members of Parliament who, when elected, appeared less than half-hearted about our cause.

Many of us felt rebellious and realised that as long as we continued to help men into Parliament who did nothing to help us, we were simply wasting our political energies. There were continuous signs that a breaking away of more urgent spirits was imminent. First some of us formed, without leaving the old suffrage organisation [NUWSS] what was known as the 'League of Practical Suffragists.' Its members pledged themselves not to work for any Parliamentary candidate who would not promise to work for and vote for any Suffrage Bill that might be brought in.

Dora Montefiore in [20], p. 40.

DOCUMENT 7 BEATRICE WEBB ENDORSES WOMEN'S
SUFFRAGE

In the following letter to Millicent Fawcett, Beatrice Webb explains that it was not a belief in 'women's rights' that converted her to the women's suffrage cause but an awareness that parliament was becoming increasingly involved with issues that were part of women's sphere, such as health, education and welfare.

My objection [to women's suffrage] was based principally on my disbelief in the validity of any 'abstract rights', whether to votes or to property ... .

I thought that women might well be content to leave the rough and tumble of party politics to their mankind, with the object of concentrating all their own energies on what seemed to me their peculiar social obligations ... .

Such a division of labour between men and women is, however, only practicable if there is among both sections alike, a continuous feeling of consent to what is being done by government ... . This consciousness of consent can hardly avoid being upset if the work of government comes actively to overlap the particular obligations of an excluded class ... . The rearing of children, the advancement of learning, and the promotion of the spiritual life – which I regard as the particular obligations of women – are, it is clear, more and more becoming the main preoccupations of the community as a whole. The legislatures of this century are, in one country after another, increasingly devoting themselves to these subjects. Whilst I rejoice in much of this new development of politics, I think it adequately accounts for the increasing restiveness of women. They are, in my opinion, rapidly losing their consciousness of consent in the work of government and are even feeling a positive obligation to take part in directing this new activity. This is, in my view, not a claim to rights or an abandonment of women's particular obligations, but a desire more effectively to fulfil their functions by sharing the control of state action in those directions.

Beatrice Webb to Mrs [Millicent] Fawcett, 5 November 1906 in Barbara Drake and Margaret Cole eds, *Our Partnership* (Cambridge University Press, 1975), pp. 362–3.

DOCUMENT 8 FAWCETT AND WSPU MILITANCY

Although reluctant to condemn WSPU militancy publicly, Millicent Fawcett believed that law and order were especially important to women and that this was being undermined by the WSPU's campaign.

I still feel disinclined to encourage one set of suffragists to denounce another set. Though I feel most strongly the essential immorality of issuing a call to the roughs of London to come and 'rush' the House of Commons ... . I feel that law and order are essential to all that makes life worth living and that they are especially and peculiarly vital to women.

Millicent Fawcett to Philippa Strachey, 12 October, 1908, The Fawcett Library, London Guildhall University, Autograph Collection, vol. 1C.

DOCUMENT 9   FAWCETT'S CASE FOR WOMEN'S SUFFRAGE

Anti-suffragists based their case on sexual difference, but Fawcett demonstrates that it could also be used to support women's suffrage.

[Anti-suffragists] ... go on repeating their catchword that 'Men are men and women are women,' meaning thereby that the point of view, the experience of life, the sphere of activity of women differ in many important respects from those of men, without seeing that these very facts are among the strongest and most irrefutable of the reasons for urging that no representative system is complete or truly national which entirely leaves out the representation of women. 'Women,' they urge '... have different duties, different capacities, the woman's being in the spheres of Home, Society, Education, Philanthropy.' One would think that the obvious conclusion from this must be that when Parliament is dealing with legislation which concerns the home, society, education, or philanthropy, it would be well if there were some constitutional means of enabling the influence and experience of the average women of the country to make themselves felt.

Millicent Garrett Fawcett, 'Men Are Men and Women Are Women', *The Englishwoman*, 1 (February 1909), pp. 17–31.

DOCUMENT 10   FAWCETT ON SEX WAR

Anti-suffragists claimed that female suffrage advocates were stirring up a sex-war but Fawcett rejected the idea.

I never believe in the possibility of a sex war. Nature has seen after that: as long as mothers have sons and fathers daughters there can never be a sex war. What draws men and women together is stronger than the brutality and tyranny drawing them apart.

Millicent Fawcett to Lady Francis Balfour, 5 March 1910, The Fawcett Library, London Guildhall University, Autograph Collection, vol. 1H1.

DOCUMENT 11   **SUFFRAGE AND SEX REFORM**

Although Christabel Pankhurst is better known for linking women's suffrage with the control of male sexuality, NUWSS members had already made this connection before Christabel took up the idea.

It will be found that everywhere the demand for women's political enfranchisement is rooted in and springs from one main fact. In ... so long as women ... are not full citizens so long must the evil continue of the double standard of morality for men and women ... .

The question of sex morality which lies deep at the root of the Women's Suffrage question is one that affects the lives of women infinitely more closely than the lives of men. As I have said, immorality is almost always accounted a sin of the worst description in a woman, while in a man it is a slight offence easily forgotten and forgiven. Now we Suffragists want to change that false view. We want to make everybody feel that it is equally wrong for both sexes to transgress the moral law. I say especially we Suffragists, because our desire to win direct political power is founded upon our belief that in that way only shall we become possessed of the power and the weapons necessary to fight this terrible evil. The Women's Movement is in fact a great Moral Movement.

Lady Chance, *Women's Suffrage and Morality: An Address to Married Women* (NUWSS, 1912), p. 6, 8–9.

DOCUMENT 12   **SUFFRAGE MILITANCY AND WOMEN'S LIBERATION**

The WSPU appealed to young women in part because it encouraged them to throw off the restrictions imposed by contemporary sex roles.

One sometimes hears people who took part in the suffrage campaign pitied ... . But for me, and for many other young women like me, militant suffrage was the very salt of life. The knowledge of it had come like a draught of fresh air into our padded, stifled lives. It gave us release of energy, it gave us that sense of being of some use in the scheme of things ... . It gave us hope of freedom and power and opportunity. It gave us scope at last, and it gave us what normal healthy youth craves – adventure and excitement.

Margaret Haig, *This Was My World* (1933) in Norquay [10], pp. 256–7.

DOCUMENT 13   SUFFRAGE MILITANCY AND THE SLAVE SPIRIT

While the NUWSS seemed narrowly concerned with women's suffrage, the WSPU encouraged a revolt against all the restrictions, in personal as well as public life, that denied women freedom.

Christabel [Pankhurst] was inspired not by pity but by a deep, secret shame – shame that any woman should tamely accept the position accorded to her as something less than an adult human being – a position half way between the child and the citizen. Christabel cared less for the political vote itself than for the dignity of her sex, and she denounced the false dignity earned by submission and extolled the true dignity accorded by revolt. She never made any secret of the fact that to her the means were even more important than the end. Militancy to her meant the putting off of the slave *spirit*.

Emmeline Pethick-Lawrence, *My Part in a Changing World* (1938) in Norquay [10], p. 63.

DOCUMENT 14   MILITANCY AND THE DOUBLE SHUFFLE

Teresa Billington Greig was one of the WSPU's most important early members but she became disillusioned with the Pankhursts.

What I condemn in militant tactics is the ... crooked course, the double shuffle between revolution and injured innocence, the playing for effects and not for results – in short, the exploitation of revolutionary forces and enthusiastic women for the purposes of advertisement. These are the things by which militancy has been degraded from revolution into political chicanery ... . The crime of the militant suffrage movement in my eyes is that it ... claims to be but is not revolution ... .

The chorus of approval ... [of early militant acts] brought out another weakness: it confirmed in us the pose of martyrdom of which we had been rather ashamed until then, and it strengthened that curious mental and moral duplicity which allowed us to engineer an outbreak and then lay the burden of its results upon the authorities ... .

The feeling within the Union against this double shuffle, this game of quick change from the garments of the rebel to those of the innocent martyr, was swamped by the public approval and extenuation of our protests ... . We were accepted into respectable circles not as rebels but as innocent victims, and as innocent victims we were led to pose.

Teresa Billington Greig, 'The Militant Suffrage Movement', in McPhee and Fitzgerald [9], pp. 138, 164–5.

DOCUMENT 15   VIOLENCE AT SUFFRAGE MEETINGS

WSPU speakers, such as Hannah Mitchell, were frequently in danger of
violent attack from males and could not be certain that the police would
protect them.

The mob played a sort of Rugby football with us. Seizing a woman they
pushed her into the arms of another group who in their turn passed her on.
An elderly reporter protected me at first, but he soon collapsed. This
frightened some of them and they drew off, but two youths held on to my
skirt so tightly that I feared it would either come off or I should be dragged
to earth on my face. But ... I turned suddenly, gave one a blow in the face
which sent him reeling down the slope, and pushed the other after him ... .
At last a group of men fought their way to me and Adela, having to beat
off our assailants with their bare fists in order to get us out of the Clough.
The crowd followed yelling like savages ... . Eventually, with a number of
men escorting us, we managed to board a tramcar, the last of the hooligans
speeding our departure with a fusillade of cabbages ... from the nearby
gardens.

Hannah Mitchell in [19], pp. 150–1.

DOCUMENT 16   BLACK FRIDAY

The following is a selection from the memorandum that the Parliamentary
Conciliation Committee for Woman Suffrage sent to the Home Office after
Black Friday with a request for a public inquiry into the conduct of the
police.

The facts which gradually came to our knowledge regarding the behaviour
of the police towards members of the Women's Social and Political Union
on November 18, 22, and 23 have induced us to collect the testimony of
women who took part in these demonstrations, and of eye-witnesses ... .
    They [the police] were instructed ... to refrain as far as possible from
making arrests. The usual course would have been ... to arrest them [the
women] on a charge of obstruction ... . The consequence [of non-arrest]
was that for many hours they were engaged in an incessant struggle with
the police. They were flung hither and thither amid moving traffic, and into
the hands of a crowd permeated by plain clothes detectives, which was
sometimes rough and indecent ... .
    We cannot resist the conclusion that the police as a whole were under the
impression that their duty was not merely to frustrate the attempts of the

women to reach the House [of Commons], but also to terrorise them in the process. They used in numerous instances excessive violence, which was at once deliberate and aggressive, and was intended to inflict injury and pain ... . They frequently handled the women with gross indecency ... .

[Participant:] 'For hours one was beaten about the body, thrown backwards and forwards from one [policeman] to another, until felt dazed from the horror of it ... . Often seized by the coat collar, dragged out of the crowd, only to be pushed helplessly along in front of one's tormentor into a side street ... where he beat one up and down the spine ...'.

The intention of terrorising and intimidating the women was carried by many of the police beyond violence. Twenty-nine [of the 135 statements submitted to the committee] complain of more or less aggravated acts of indecency [by the police].

[Participant:] 'Several times constables and plain clothes men who were in the crowd passed their arms around me from the back and clutched hold of my breasts in as public a manner as possible, and the men in the crowd followed their example ...'.

H. N. Brailsford, Secretary of the Parliamentary Conciliation Committee for Woman Suffrage, 'Treatment of the Women's Deputations By the Police', 18 February 1911, PRO, HO 144/1106/200455.

DOCUMENT 17   FAWCETT ON WSPU MILITANCY

Fawcett grew increasingly frustrated with WSPU militant acts which undermined the NUWSS's efforts to build support for suffrage legislation.

I do think these personal assaults perfectly abominable and above all extraordinarily silly. The P. M.'s [Prime Minister's] statement on the 22nd was not just exactly all we wanted but it was better than anything that had ever been offered us before and was at any rate good enough to make *The Times* say the next day that it had made W. S. [women's suffrage] a question definitely before the country at this election and that if there is a Liberal majority it will be a mandate to grant suffrage to women. And then these idiots go out smashing windows and bashing ministers' hats over their eyes.

Millicent Fawcett to Lady Francis Balfour, 28 November 1910. The Fawcett Library, London Guildhall University, Autograph Collection, vol. 1H3.

DOCUMENT 18   **FORCED FEEDING**

Mary Richardson, one of the suffragettes who was force-fed, described what it was like in her autobiography.

The following morning horror of forcible feeding was announced by the rumbling of the wheels of the trolley approaching my cell door. I sat down on the floor and pushed my arms under and round the hot-water pipe. I intended to resist to the utmost. As I sat and waited five wardresses came in. They succeeded in loosening my hands and arm from round the pipe; and, when they had done this, they tried to lay me flat on the floor. I struggled with them. By the time I was on my back we were all breathless and panting. To my horror, then, four of the wardresses, who were all hefty women, lay across my legs and body to keep me pinned to the floor. And now that the victim was trussed up and ready the doctors came in dragging the hated trolley at their heels. One knelt to grip my shoulders, another lifted aloft the funnel that was to receive the liquid, the third knelt by my head and took the long tube in his hand and, little by little, forced the stiff nozzle at the end of the tube up my left nostril. As the nozzle turned at the top of my nose to enter my gullet it seemed as if my left eye was being wrenched out of its socket. Then the food, a mixture of cocoa, Bovril, medicines and a drug to keep one from vomiting when the tube was drawn out, was poured into the funnel and down into my aching, bruised, quivering body ... . After ten weeks of forcible feeding I was released, little better than a breathing corpse.

Mary R. Richardson in [27], p. 84.

DOCUMENT 19   **SEX AND SUFFRAGE**

In the last years before the First World War, Christabel Pankhurst argued that women needed the vote to protect themselves against male sexual abuse.

The sexual diseases are the great causes of physical, mental, and moral degeneracy, and of race suicide. As they are very widespread (from 75 to 80 per cent. of men being infected by gonorrhoea, and a considerable percentage, difficult to ascertain precisely, being infected with syphilis), the problem is one of appalling magnitude.

To discuss an evil, and then to run away from it without suggesting how it may be cured, is not the way of the Suffragettes, and in the following pages will be found a proposed cure for the great evil in question. That cure, briefly stated, is Votes for Women and Chastity for men ... .

Regulation of vice and enforced medical inspection of the White Slaves is equally futile, and gives a false appearance of security which is fatal. Chastity for men – or, in other words, their observance of the same moral standard as is observed by women – is therefore indispensable.

The knowledge of what the Hidden Scourge really is, and of how multitudes of women are the victims of it, will put a new and great passion into the movement for political enfranchisement. It will make that movement more than ever akin to all previous wars against slavery ... .

The cause of sexual disease is the subjection of women. Therefore to destroy the one we must destroy the other. Viewed in the light of that fact, Mr. Asquith's opposition to votes for women is seen to be an over-whelming public danger ... .

The demand for Votes for Women means a revolt against wrongs of many kinds – against social injustice and political mismanagement ... . But more than all it is a revolt against the evil system under which women are regarded as sub-human and as the sex-slaves of men.

Christabel Pankhurst, *The Great Scourge and How to End It* (1913) in Marcus [8], pp. 188–9, 194, 234.

DOCUMENT 20   ASQUITH AND SUFFRAGE REFORM

When he met with the ELF deputation in 1914, Prime Minister Asquith gave the following response to their demand for women's suffrage.

On one point I am in complete agreement with you. I have always said that if you are going to give the franchise to women, give it to them on the same terms as to men. Make it a democratic measure. It is no good paltering with it. If the discrimination of sex does not justify the giving of the vote to one sex and withholding it from the other it follows *a fortiori* that the discrimination of sex does not justify and cannot warrant giving to women a restricted form of franchise while you give to men an unrestricted form of franchise. If a change is to come, it must be democratic in its basis.

The Suffragette, 26 June, 1914, p. 178.

DOCUMENT 21   RATHBONE AND THE ELECTION
FIGHTING FUND

Eleanor Rathbone was one of the strongest opponents within the NUWSS of its alliance with the Labour Party and its Election Fighting Fund policy.

The proposed Anti-government policy of the N. U. [NUWSS] will, if adopted, start it definitely on a path of what may be called constitutional coercion, as opposed to its previous record of constitutional persuasion. A step in that direction has already been taken by the formation of the Election Fighting Fund. We shall thus be moving one step nearer to the militancy of the W.S.P.U. and the [Women's] Freedom League ... .

Already the Anti-Government policy of the W.S.P.U. has done something to create an impression, which hitherto the N. U. has done its best to counteract, of antagonism between Women's Suffrage and Liberalism. In [the] future, if the new policy is adopted, all Suffrage Societies will combine to strengthen that impression ... .

Apart from its effectiveness as an instrument of coercion, the new policy raises several difficult questions. First, we talk of shortening the present Government's term of office. But ... the trend of by-elections makes it more probable that the Conservatives will come into power next Parliament. If they do ... I think it is pretty clear what to expect. We know that a far smaller proportion of Unionists are suffragists than of Liberals ... .

Eleanor Rathbone, 'The Gentle Art of Making Enemies: A Criticism of the Proposed Policy of the National Union', n. d. (1913). The Fawcett Library, London Guildhall University, NUWS Papers, 2/NWS/B1/3.

DOCUMENT 22   SUFFRAGISTS AND THE PEACE MOVEMENT

Lord Cecil's warning against any NUWSS association with the peace movement probably reinforced Fawcett's own views on this matter.

Permit me to express my great regret that you should have thought it right not only to take part in the 'peace' meeting last night but also to have allowed the organization of the National Union [NUWSS] to be used for its promotion. Actions of that kind will undoubtedly make it very difficult for the friends of Women's Suffrage in both the Unionist and Ministerial [Liberal] parties.

Even to me the action seems so unreasonable under the circumstances as to shake my belief in the fitness of Women to deal with the great Territorial questions and I can only console myself by the belief that in this matter the National Union do not represent the opinions of their fellow countrywomen.

Lord Robert Cecil to Mrs Henry Fawcett, 5 August 1914, The Fawcett Library, London Guildhall University, Fawcett Autograph Collection, vol. 1K.

DOCUMENT 23   **THE SPLIT IN THE NUWSS**

The 1915 split in the NUWSS was especially bitter because those who resigned believed the NUWSS was repudiating the prewar conviction that women would fundamentally transform politics.

The real cleavage of opinion in the Union [NUWSS] lies between those who consider it essential to work for the vote simply as a political tool, and those who believe that the demand for the vote should be linked with the advocacy of the deeper principles which underlie it.

This cleavage of opinion was clearly shown at the Council meeting, when a ... majority ... passed a number of resolutions founded upon the belief that 'the Women's Suffrage movement is based on the principle that social relations should be governed not by physical force but by recognition of mutual rights.' They were, however, not prepared to give effect to this decision ... .

Do we ask for the vote merely as a political tool, or do we wish the National Union to link it with the advocacy of the deeper principles, the consciousness of which has been the source of so much vigor and impassioned devotion to our workers? ...

The [resigning members] ... believe that the Union cannot survive as a living organisation with the driving power of ideals behind it unless, at this tremendous crisis, it recognises the great principles for which it stands, and continues to uphold the ideal of the supremacy of moral force in human affairs. To this belief the N. U. has indeed already testified in its declaration against [WSPU] militancy.

Catherine Marshall *et. al*, 'Statement By Retiring Members and Others', *The Common Cause*, 4 June, 1915, pp. 121–2.

DOCUMENT 24 THE SPEAKERS' CONFERENCE AND
WOMEN'S SUFFRAGE

W. H. Dickinson, one of the main women's suffrage advocates in the Speakers' Conference, was very concerned that the suffrage societies might reject the conference's proposals because they did not include equal franchise rights for women.

I hope that you will not let the W. S. [Women's Suffrage] Societies rush to the conclusion that our [Speakers'] conference has done nothing for the cause. I think that when the recommendations appear you will find that you have something very substantial ... only please do all you can to induce women to see that it will be bad tactics to fall foul of the conference because it may not have done all that they expected. The whole matter will need the most careful handling so as to avoid the risk of the Government having an excuse for saying that as it is impossible to satisfy the advocates of W. S. they refrain from dealing with W. S. at all.

W. H. Dickinson to Mrs Henry Fawcett, 19 January 1917. The Fawcett Library, London Guildhall University, Autograph Collection, vol. 1L.

DOCUMENT 25 THE ORIGIN OF THE AGE RESTRICTION
FOR WOMEN VOTERS

In a private meeting with the NUWSS's spokesmen in the Speakers' Conference, Millicent Fawcett agreed to the imposition of an age limit for female voters as part of a compromise proposal to be introduced at the conference.

Sir John Simon and Mr. Dickinson both considered there was a good chance of the [Speakers'] Conference recommending Women's Suffrage. The difficulty and danger would arise when concrete proposals for Women's Suffrage came to be discussed. The two Members of Parliament thought there was little or no chance of Adult Suffrage being recommended by the Conference and that for the Adultists to press for it would risk the loss of even a general recommendation for Women's Suffrage in any form .... A good deal of talk took place about various ways of dealing with the excess of women over men. Finally I think there was a general agreement that raising the voting age for women was the least objectionable way of reducing the number of women.

Millicent Fawcett, 'Memorandum on conversation at Sir John Simon's house', 15 December, 1916 [included with NUWSS Executive Committee

Minutes, 4 January, 1917]. The Fawcett Library, London Guildhall Univesity, NUWSS Papers, 2/NWS/A1/9.

DOCUMENT 26   **THE NUWSS REACTION TO THE SPEAKERS' CONFERENCE PROPOSALS**

Many suffrage reformers were dissatisfied with the Speakers' Conference proposals for women's suffrage because they excluded most female factory workers.

Miss [Eleanor] Rathbone thought that the [Speakers' Conference] recommendations were not at all satisfactory as such a Franchise would be of no use to the [female] factory worker. We had been pressing for the Franchise on account of the industrial dislocation to be expected after the War. This basis would only enfranchise the wives of Trade Unionists who would vote with the men. She thought we might have to yield to it, but it seemed like throwing over the [female] factory worker altogether.

Mrs. Strachey thought that the basis was thoroughly unsatisfactory, but that as it had been accepted by the Speakers' Conference there was a strong presumption that it would also be accepted by the House … . We stand a chance of really getting something … now, and opposition to it based on however good reasons might wreck the chance altogether.

NUWSS Executive Committee minutes, 1 February, 1917. The Fawcett Library, London Guildhall University, NUWSS Papers, 2/NWS/A1/9.

DOCUMENT 27   **THE SUFFRAGE SOCIETIES DEPUTATION TO THE PRIME MINISTER**

When the deputation from the women's suffrage societies met with the prime minister, Millicent Fawcett assured him they would accept the government's proposals rather than insisting on equal franchise rights but other members of the deputation reminded him that female munitions workers would remain disenfranchised under the government's scheme.

[Millicent Fawcett] I think I may say … that we shall be very gratified if … the Prime Minister should see his way to improve, in a democratic direction, upon the recommendations of the Conference – but only so far as is consistent with the safety of the whole scheme … . We should greatly prefer an imperfect scheme that can pass, to the most perfect scheme in the world that could not pass.

[Mary Macarthur] Women munition workers have asked me to say on their behalf that they do not ask for the vote as a reward for [wartime] services rendered ... . They ask it because they want to play their part in the great reconstruction work that is lying ahead of us all. We know ... there is no class which will be more affected ... by reconstruction proposals than the women who have come into industry ... during this emergency ... . We feel bound to point out to you that the proposals of the Speakers' Conference shut the door against the vast majority of women engaged on munition work ... .

'Women's Suffrage Deputation March 29, 1917', House of Lords Record Office, Lloyd George Papers, F/229/3.

DOCUMENT 28   THE CASE FOR EQUAL FRANCHISE

Eva Hubback was the NUSEC's parliamentary secretary in the 1920s.

It has become increasingly clear, election after election, that the woman who was enfranchised [in 1918] was either the married woman ... or the woman of property ... . The ... situation thus became clear: it was the women occupied in industry and in the professions ... who by the terms of the [1918] measure were shut out from its advantages. It has been estimated, indeed, that only about one in fifteen of the women wage-earners have the right to vote. The great majority of women in industry leave before they are thirty to get married, while those over thirty in many cases live either with their families, or in furnished rooms, big hostels, etc. It is a matter of common knowledge that comparatively few professional women ... are the proud possessors of houses, or even of unfurnished rooms of their own. The importance of this becomes manifest if we remember that almost every year Parliament is discussing legislation ... dealing with the conditions of ... women workers ... . In certain cases the interests of women workers clash with those of men ... . It certainly cannot be right that the labour of adult women should be controlled by a Parliament which is not responsible to those whose livelihood it is directing.

Eva Hubback, 'The Case For Equal Franchise', *Fortnightly Review*, CXXIII (April 1928), p. 529.

DOCUMENT 29   CONSERVATIVE WOMEN DEMAND FRANCHISE REFORM

Although the Conservative Party's women's organization was divided over what reform should be introduced, they insisted that action by the government was necessary.

There is undoubtedly a growing feeling [among Conservative Party women] that if the Government do not see their way to appointing the Conference [on franchise reform], or to appointing it in such time as will allow of its finding becoming operative at the next Election, it will do us a lot of harm when that time comes.

There is no question of the merits of the case being involved and the opinion of Unionist women differs widely on the subject, but even among those who differ there seems to be a great measure of agreement that a promise has been made that the subject shall be dealt with, and that it will be very disastrous if the Prime Minister can be represented at the Election as not having redeemed a Pledge.

We [Conservative Party] depend at Elections upon masses of women with few really definite convictions, whose instincts are in the main naturally conservative but who might easily be swept away if their faith in the sanctity of the Prime Minister's pledges were shaken by skilful manoeuvres on the part of the enemy.

Gwendolen, Lady Elveden to Colonel [F. S.] Jackson [Conservative Party Chairman], 16 November 1926. PRO, HO 45/13020.

DOCUMENT 30   CONSERVATIVE PARTY OFFICIALS ON EQUAL FRANCHISE

Although willing, with some reluctance, to accept equal franchise at age 25, the Conservative Party's Central Office warned that lowering it to 21 would significantly damage the party's electoral prospects.

It must I suppose be accepted as certain that the Government are committed to the introduction of a Bill to equalise the franchise for men and women. If this is not so, and there is still room for argument on the political question, we are decidedly of the opinion that the reduction of the franchise age in the case of women to 21 would have a detrimental effect on the fortunes of the Party. In ... the industrial areas, particularly in those districts where women work in the mills, it is believed that such a measure would bring on to the electoral rolls a large majority of votes for the Labour Party, by reason of their being under the influence of the Trade Union officials.

We [Conservative Party Central Office] believe that if the age of franchise for women was reduced to 25, it would be politically better for the Conservative Party than 21, as particularly in the North of England, a large proportion of the women of 25 would be married and, therefore, much less likely to be led astray by extravagant theories.

Conservative Party Central Office memorandum presented to the Cabinet Equal Franchise Committee on 21 February 1927. PRO, CAB 27/336.

DOCUMENT 31 THE CABINET CONSIDERS EQUAL FRANCHISE LEGISLATION

Although the Cabinet preferred to grant equal franchise at age 25, it reluctantly accepted Baldwin's view that women's voting age be lowered to 21.

At the Cabinet Stanley [Baldwin] opened with a short resume of the position with regard to our pledges on the women's vote concluding that the only thing we could do was to give it all round at 21. Winston [Churchill] led the opposition with great vehemence and our opinions were then taken all the way round. I took the view with many others that 25 for both sexes would be preferable but did not think we should see it through and therefore favoured 21 and without a conference beforehand. I did not think that we should lose particularly from the party point of view ... . In the end 21 without a conference prevailed by a considerable majority. Winston very unhappy as indeed were also F. E. [Smith, Lord Birkenhead] and several others.

Leo Amery diary, 12 April 1927 in John Barnes and D. Nicholson eds, *The Leo Amery Diaries, vol. 1: 1896–1929*, Hutchinson, 1980, p. 491.

DOCUMENT 32 THE CASE AGAINST EQUAL FRANCHISE

Even after Baldwin announced the government's intention to introduce equal franchise legislation, some Conservatives continued to oppose the reform, warning that it would enfranchise young women who were likely to be feminists.

It cannot be said that this announcement [by Baldwin of an equal franchise bill] was received with enthusiasm, either by the supporters of the

Government in the House, or by the Conservative Party, as a whole, in the country. Despite the strenuous and skilful propaganda issued by the Conservative central office, the Government's proposals received only very lukewarm support at the Cardiff [Conservative Party] Conference of 1927.

One effect, and that the most important effect, of the measure is that it will place for all time the women voters in a majority, not only in the country as a whole, but in practically every constituency ... .

So far, it is true, there have been no signs of the formation of a feminist party, but one result of this Bill will be to increase enormously the number of unmarried women on the [election] register, and a small, but determined, feminist group, interested solely in feminist questions, might easily dominate the situation in those constituencies where the cleavage on normal political lines is into parties of approximately equal strength. The increase in the number of unmarried women voters will probably facilitate the formation of such groups.

"Backbencher", 'The Franchise Bill', *The English Review*, 46 (April 1928), pp. 394–5.

DOCUMENT 33   **THE SUFFRAGE SOCIETIES DEPUTATION TO THE PRIME MINISTER**

When the deputation from the suffrage organizations met with the prime minister, they did not base their case for equal franchise on the idea that women were entitled to equal rights but claimed that employed women constituted an important economic group that was unable to use the ballot to defend its economic interests.

[Eleanor Rathbone] I desire only to make a single point. The great majority of women who work for their living, in industries or professions, are among the disenfranchised. Every year Parliament considers Bills, such as your own Factories Bill ... which vitally affect the conditions under which those women earn their livings ... . Whatever the merits of this legislation, it is dangerous that the women it concerns should be without the means of influencing Parliament which male workers possess. There is rivalry between men and women workers in many occupations. It cannot be said that in this matter the already enfranchised women adequately represent the unenfranchised. The majority of the enfranchised are wives and mothers, who may look at these questions of sex competition from the point of view of their husbands and sons, rather than of their unenfranchised sisters.

'Notes of Deputation from the Equal Political Rights Campaign Committee', 14 March 1927. PRO, CAB 24/185/90.

CHRONOLOGY

1866   Women's suffrage petition presented to Parliament by
           John Stuart Mill.

1867   National Society for Women's Suffrage formed.

1871   London National Society for Women's Suffrage splits from
           other suffrage societies.

1872   Central Committee of National Society for Women's
           Suffrage founded.

1877   New Central Committee of National Society for Women's
           Suffrage established.

1888   Central Committee of National Society for Women's
           Suffrage splits away from Central National Committee.

1889   Women's Franchise League formed.

1897   National Union of Women's Suffrage Societies created.

1903   Women's Social and Political Union founded.

1906   Liberal Party wins the general election.

1907   Women's Freedom League established.

1909   People's Suffrage Federation formed.

1910   All-party Conciliation Committee created.

1912   NUWSS-Labour Party alliance established.

1914
(June)   ELF deputation to Prime Minister Asquith.

1914
(July)   First World War begins.

1916   Speaker's Conference on electoral reform appointed.

1918   Representation of the People Act extends the vote to
       women aged 30 and above who were also local electors
       or the wives of local government electors.

1928   Representation of the People (Equal Franchise) Act
       enfranchises women aged 21 and over.

GLOSSARY

PEOPLE

Astor, Nancy (1879–1964): in 1919 Astor became the first female member of the House of Commons. She established the Consultative Committee of Women's Organisations in 1921 to develop an agreed feminist reform programme. Astor was the key female within the Conservative Party lobbying for equal franchise in the 1920s.

Becker, Lydia (1827–1890): after serving as secretary of the Manchester Society for Women's Suffrage, Becker became the first secretary of the National Society for Women's Suffrage. She remained its leader and edited the *Women's Suffrage Journal* until the late 1880s.

Billington Greig, Teresa (1877–1964): an ILP organizer who also became one of the WSPU's first organizers. She was one of the leaders of the revolt against the Pankhursts when they broke with the ILP, and became a leader of the Women's Freedom League.

Despard, Charlotte (1844–1939): a WSPU member who withdrew when it broke with the ILP. One of the founders of the Women's Freedom League, she became its first president.

Fawcett, Millicent Garrett (1847–1929): Fawcett became a member of the London Society for Women's Suffrage's executive when it was formed in 1867 and was the leader of the NUWSS from its formation in 1897. Although reluctant to publicly criticize WSPU militant methods, she insisted the NUWSS rely on constitutional methods and privately believed WSPU militancy after 1910 was undermining the NUWSS's efforts to win converts to the suffrage cause.

Marshall, Catherine (1880–1961): Marshall was an important leader of the 'democratic suffragists' within the NUWSS. She became the NUWSS's parliamentary secretary in 1911 and was appointed secretary of the Election Fighting Fund Committee when it was established in 1912.

Pankhurst, Christabel (1880–1958): Emmeline Pankhurst's eldest daughter. One of the earliest WSPU members, she introduced militant methods into the WSPU suffrage campaign. After 1907 she and her mother emerged as the dominant figures within the WSPU.

Pankhurst, Emmeline (1858–1928): founded the WSPU in 1903 and was always its spiritual leader although her daughter Christabel assumed greater responsibility for directing the WSPU campaign after 1910. Repeatedly imprisoned during the suffrage campaign, she inspired many women to join the suffrage movement by her willingness to sacrifice her life if necessary for the cause.

Pankhurst, Sylvia (1882–1960): Emmeline Pankhurst's younger daughter. Although she remained in the WSPU when her mother and her sister Christabel broke with the ILP, she disagreed with their policy and sought to link feminism and socialism. Expelled from the WSPU by Christabel in 1914, she formed her own organization, the East London Federation of the Suffragettes.

Rathbone, Eleanor (1872–1946): Rathbone became the Liverpool Women's Suffrage Society's secretary in 1897, and later became a member of the NUWSS executive. Elected president of the NUSEC in 1919, Rathbone directed the campaign for equal franchise in the 1920s.

Rhondda, Viscountess [Margaret Haig Thomas] (1883–1958): a member of the Women's Social and Political Union who was imprisoned briefly for setting fire to letterboxes. In 1921 she founded the Six Point Group to work for feminist reforms. Dissatisfied with the lack of progress toward equal franchise, she formed the Equal Political Rights Campaign Committee in 1926 in an attempt to ginger up the campaign.

Roper, Esther (1868–1938): Roper was secretary of the Manchester National Society for Women's Suffrage (later the North of England Society for Women's Suffrage) from 1893 to 1905. She was responsible for recruiting working-class women into the suffrage movement at a time when its members were mainly middle- and upper-class women.

ORGANISATIONS

Conservative and Unionist Women's Franchise Association established in 1907 with Lady Selborne as president. Comprising Conservative Party women, it attempted to convert Conservatives to the suffrage cause.

East London Federation of the Women's Social and Political Union established in 1912 by Sylvia Pankhurst. When Sylvia refused to accept Christabel Pankhurst's anti-male policy, she was expelled from the WSPU and in 1914 the organization changed its name to the East London Federation of the Suffragettes.

Election Fighting Fund Committee established by the NUWSS in 1912 to implement the NUWSS's electoral alliance with the Labour Party. Its formation represented a triumph for the NUWSS leaders from the north of England who wished the NUWSS to become part of a more radical, 'democratic suffragist' movement. Catherine Marshall, a leading proponent within the NUWSS of closer ties with the Labour Party, became secretary of the committee.

Equal Political Rights Demonstration Committee an umbrella organization established in 1926 with Lady Rhondda as its leader. Dissatisfied with the lack of progress toward equal franchise, Rhondda believed more militant tactics were needed. After sponsoring a mass demonstration in July 1926, the committee changed its name to the Equal Political Rights Campaign Committee.

London Society for Women's Service chaired by Clementia Taylor, the London National Society for Women's Suffrage was established in 1867. After several name changes it was renamed the London Society for Women's Suffrage in 1907 and became the London Society for Women's Service in 1919. In 1953 it became the Fawcett Society.

National Society for Women's Suffrage established in 1867 by representatives of the London National Society for Women's Suffrage and the Manchester National Society for Women's Suffrage following the defeat of the women's suffrage amendment to the 1867 Reform Bill. It was a loose federation intended to co-ordinate the efforts of the regional suffrage societies. Lydia Becker, the Manchester Society's secretary, became its secretary.

National Union of Societies for Equal Citizenship the National Union of Women's Suffrage Societies changed its name to the National Union of Societies for Equal Citizenship in 1919 to reflect its expanded reform programme. Eleanor Rathbone was its president from 1919 to 1928. It was primarily responsible for conducting the feminist campaign for equal franchise in the 1920s.

National Union of Women's Suffrage Societies established in 1897. Although Millicent Fawcett was not formally elected president until 1907, she was viewed as the NUWSS's leader from its beginning. In 1909 the NUWSS began publishing its own journal, *The Common Cause*, which had a circulation of 10,000 by 1912.

North of England Society for Women's Suffrage the new name given to the Manchester National Society for Women's Suffrage when it affiliated to the National Union of Women's Suffrage Societies in 1897. With Esther Roper as its secretary, it was especially concerned with drawing working-class women into the suffrage movement.

People's Suffrage Federation established in 1908 by women trade unionists and Women's Co-operative Guild members. Led by Margaret Llewelyn Davies, the WCG's secretary, it advocated adult suffrage in order that working-class women would gain the right to vote.

Standing Joint Committee of Industrial Women's Organisations established in February 1916 by women's organizations concerned that female workers were being used by employers to undercut male wage rates. Chaired by Mary Macarthur, National Federation of Women Workers' secretary, it included representatives from the major working-class women's organizations such as the Women's Co-operative Guild and the Women's Labour League. It became the Labour Party's Women's Advisory Committee in 1918.

Women's Freedom League established in 1907 by WSPU members who opposed the Pankhursts' split with the Labour movement. Charlotte Despard became its president. Its journal, *The Vote*, was issued from 1909 to 1933.

Women's Liberal Federation established in 1887. Although Catherine (Mrs William) Gladstone became its first president, Eva McClaren was its national organizer and the real moving spirit within the organization. Although some of its founders were the wives of Liberal MPs who thought the main function of the WLF should be to help their husbands gain election, the majority of WLF members believed it should help elect Liberals who supported women's causes, such as suffrage and temperance.

Women's National Anti-Suffrage League established in 1908. Although Lady Jersey chaired its executive committee, Mrs Humphrey Ward, the popular novelist, was the real driving force within the organization. It merged with the men's anti-suffrage league later in 1908 and became the National League for Opposing Women's Suffrage.

Women's Social and Political Union established in 1903 by Emmeline Pankhurst. It used militant methods which led its members to be called 'suffragettes' to distinguish them from the constitutional suffragists. Its journal, *Votes for Women*, reached a peak circulation of almost 40,000 in 1909–10.

BIBLIOGRAPHY

PRIMARY SOURCES

A. Microforms

1   'Consultative Committee of Women's Organisations Minutes', in *The Records of the Women's Joint Congressional Committee*, Library of Congress, microfilm.
2   *Women, Politics and Welfare: The Papers of Nancy Astor, 1879–1964*, Adam Matthew, microfilm.
3   *Women, Suffrage and Politics: The Papers of Sylvia Pankhurst, 1882–1960*. Adam Matthew, microfilm.
4   *Women's Social and Political Emancipation: The Suffragette Fellowship Collection in the Museum of London*, Harvester, microfilm.
5   *Women's Suffrage Collection from Manchester Central Library*, Adam Matthew, microfilm.

B. Document Collections

6   Hollis, P. (ed.), *Women in Public 1850–1900*, Allen and Unwin, 1979.
7   Lewis, J. (ed.), *Before the Vote Was Won: Arguments for and Against Women's Suffrage*, Routledge, 1987.
8   Marcus, J. (ed.), *Suffrage and the Pankhursts*, Routledge, 1987.
9   McPhee, C. and A. FitzGerald (eds), *The Non-Violent Militant: Selected Writings of Teresa Billington-Greig*, Routledge, 1987.
10 Norquay, G. (ed.), *Voices and Votes: A Literary Anthology of the Women's Suffrage Campaign*, Manchester University Press, 1995.

C. Writings By Participants

11 Cook, B. (ed.), *Crystal Eastman On Women and Revolution*, Oxford University Press, 1978.
12 Fawcett, M., *What I Remember*, T. Fisher Unwin, 1924.
13 Fawcett, M., *The Women's Victory – and After: Personal Reminiscences, 1911–1918*, Sidgwick and Jackson, 1920.
14 Gawthorpe, M., *Up Hill To Holloway*, Traversity Press, 1962.

15   Hubback, E., 'The Case for Equal Franchise', *Fortnightly Review*, 123, April, 1928.
16   Jones, H. (ed.), *Duty and Citizenship: The Correspondence and Political Papers of Violet Markham, 1896–1953*, The Historians Press, 1994.
17   Kenney, A., *Memories of a Militant*, Edward Arnold, 1924.
18   Mackworth, M., *This Was My World*, Macmillan, 1933.
19   Mitchell, H., *The Hard Way Up*, Faber and Faber, 1968.
20   Montefiore, D., *From a Victorian to a Modern*, E. Archer, 1927.
21   Pankhurst, C., *Unshackled: The Story of How We Won the Vote, Hutchinson, 1959.*
22   Pankhurst, E. S., *The Suffragette Movement*, Longman, 1931.
23   Pankhurst, E., *My Own Story*, Eveleigh Nash, 1914.
24   Pethick-Lawrence, E., *My Part in a Changing World*, Victor Gollancz, 1938.
25   Rathbone, E., 'Changes in Public Life', in R. Strachey (ed.), *Our Freedom and Its Results*, Hogarth Press, 1936.
26   Rathbone, E., *Milestones: Presidential Addresses*, NUSEC, 1929.
27   Richardson, M., *Laugh a Defiance*, Weidenfeld and Nicolson, 1953.
28   Strachey, R., *The Cause*, G. Bell, 1928.
29   Strachey, R., *Millicent Garrett Fawcett*, John Murray, 1931.
30   Thompson, W., *An Appeal to One-Half the Human Race*, Longman, Hurst, Rees, 1825.

SECONDARY SOURCES

A. Books

31   Alberti, J., *Beyond Suffrage: Feminists in War and Peace, 1914–28*, Macmillan, 1989.
32   Alberti, J., *Eleanor Rathbone*, Sage, 1996.
33   Barrow, M., *Women 1870–1928: A Select Guide to Printed and Archival Sources in the United Kingdom*, Mansell, 1981.
34   Bolt, C., *The Women's Movements in the United States and Britain from the 1790s to the 1920s*, University of Massachusetts Press, 1993.
35   Burton, A., *Burdens of History: British Feminists, Indian Women, and Imperial Culture, 1865–1915*, University of North Carolina Press, 1994.
36   Butler, D., *The Electoral System in Britain Since 1918*, Clarendon Press, 1963.
37   Caine, B., *English Feminism 1780–1980*, Oxford University Press, 1997.
38   Caine, B., *Victorian Feminists*, Oxford University Press, 1992.
39   Chew, D., *The Life and Writings of Ada Neild Chew*, Virago, 1982.

40 Collette, C., *For Labour and for Women: The Women's Labour League, 1906–1918*, Manchester University Press, 1989.

41 Cook, K. and N. Evans, '"The Petty Antics of the Bell-Ringing Band"? The Women's Suffrage Movement in Wales, 1890–1918', in A. John (ed.), *Our Mothers' Land: Chapters in Welsh Women's History, 1830–1939*, University of Wales Press, 1991.

42 Eoff, S., *Viscountess Rhondda, Equalitarian Feminist*, Ohio State University Press, 1991.

43 Gaffin, J. and D. Thoms, *Caring and Sharing: The Centenary History of the Co-operative Women's Guild*, Co-operative Union, 1983.

44 Fletcher, S., *Maude Royden: A Life*, Basil Blackwell, 1989.

45 Fulford, R., *Votes for Women*, Faber and Faber, 1957.

46 Garner, L., *A Brave and Beautiful Spirit: Dora Marsden 1882–1960*, Gower, 1990.

47 Garner, L., *Stepping Stones to Women's Liberty: Feminist Ideas in the Women's Suffrage Movement 1900–1918*, Gower, 1984.

48 Gorham, D., *Vera Brittain*, Blackwell, 1996.

49 Graves, P., *Labour Women: Women in British Working-Class Politics 1918–1939*, Cambridge University Press, 1994.

50 Hannam, J., *Isabella Ford*, Basil Blackwell, 1989.

51 Harrison, B., *Peaceable Kingdom*, Clarendon Press, 1982.

52 Harrison, B., *Prudent Revolutionaries: Portraits of British Feminists between the Wars*, Clarendon Press, 1987.

53 Harrison, B., *Separate Spheres: The Opposition to Women's Suffrage in Britain*, Holmes and Meirer, 1978.

54 Harrison, B., 'Women's Suffrage at Westminster', in M. Bentley and J. Stevenson (eds), *High and Low Politics in Modern Britain*, Oxford University Press, 1983.

55 Heeney, B., *The Women's Movement in the Church of England 1850–1930*, Clarendon Press, 1988.

56 Herstein, S., *A Mid-Victorian Feminist, Barbara Leigh Smith Bodichon*, Yale University Press, 1985.

57 Hollis, P., *Ladies Elect: Women in English Local Government 1865–1914*, Clarendon Press, 1987.

58 Holton, S., *Feminism and Democracy: Women's Suffrage and Reform Politics in Britain 1900–1918*, Cambridge University Press, 1986.

59 Holton, S., 'From Anti-Slavery to Suffrage Militancy: The Bright Circle, Elizabeth Cady Stanton and the British Women's Movement', in C. Daley and M. Nolan (eds), *Suffrage and Beyond: International Feminist Perspectives*, New York University Press, 1994.

60 Holton, S., '"In Sorrowful Wrath": Suffrage Militancy and the Romantic Feminism of Emmeline Pankhurst', in H. Smith (ed.), *British Feminism in the Twentieth Century*, Edward Elgar, 1990.

61 Holton, S., *Suffrage Days*, Routledge, 1996.

62 Hume, L., *The National Union of Women's Suffrage Societies 1897–1914*, Garland, 1982.

63   Hunt, K., *Equivocal Feminists: The Social Democratic Federation and the Woman Question 1884–1911*, Cambridge University Press, 1996.

64   Jalland, P., *Women, Marriage and Politics 1860–1914*, Oxford University Press, 1986.

65   Jarvis, D., 'The Conservative Party and the Politics of Gender, 1900–1939', in M. Francis and I. Zweiniger-Bargielowska (eds), *The Conservatives and British Society, 1880–1990*, University of Wales Press, 1996.

66   Jarvis, D., 'The Shaping of Conservative Electoral Hegemony, 1918–39', in J. Lawrence and M. Taylor (eds), *Party, State and Society: Electoral Behaviour in Britain since 1820*, Scolar Press, 1997.

67   Joannou, M. and J. Purvis (eds), *The Women's Suffrage Movement: New Feminist Perspectives*, Manchester University Press, 1998.

68   John, A., *Elizabeth Robins: Staging a Life 1862–1952*, Routledge, 1995.

69   John, A. and C. Eustance (eds), *The Men's Share? Masculinities, Male Support and Women's Suffrage in Britain, 1890–1920*, Routledge, 1997.

70   Kamm, J., *Rapiers and Battleaxes: The Women's Movement and its Aftermath*, Allen and Unwin, 1966.

71   Kean, H., *Deeds Not Words: The Lives of Suffragette Teachers*, Pluto Press, 1990.

72   Kent, S., *Making Peace: The Reconstruction of Gender in Interwar Britain*, Princeton University Press, 1993.

73   Kent, S., *Sex and Suffrage in Britain, 1860–1914*, Princeton University Press, 1987.

74   Law, C., *Suffrage and Power: The Women's Movement 1918–1928*, I. B. Tauris, 1997.

75   Leneman, L., *A Guid Cause: The Women's Movement in Scotland*, Aberdeen University Press, 1991.

76   Levine, P., *Feminist Lives in Victorian England*, Basil Blackwell, 1990.

77   Levine, P., *Victorian Feminism 1850–1900*, Hutchinson, 1987.

78   Lewis, G., *Eva Gore-Booth and Esther Roper*, Pandora, 1988.

79   Lewis, J., *Women and Social Action in Victorian and Edwardian England*, Edward Elgar, 1991.

80   Liddington, J., *The Life and Times of a Respectable Rebel: Selina Cooper 1864–1946*, Virago, 1984.

81   Liddington, J. and J. Norris, *One Hand Tied Behind Us: The Rise of the Women's Suffrage Movement*, Virago, 1978.

82   Liddington, J., *The Road to Greenham Common: Feminism and Anti-Militarism in Britain since 1820*, Virago, 1989.

83   Linklater, E., *An Unhusbanded Life, Charlotte Despard: Suffragette, Socialist and Sinn Feiner*, Hutchinson, 1980.

84   Melman, B., *Women and the Popular Imagination in the Twenties*, Macmillan, 1988.

85 Mitchell, D., *The Fighting Pankhursts: A Study in Tenacity*, Cape, 1967.

86 Mitchell, D., *Queen Christabel: A Biography of Christabel Pankhurst*, Macdonald and Jane, 1977.

87 Morgan, D., *Suffragists and Liberals: The Politics of Women's Suffrage in Britain*, Blackwell, 1975.

88 Mulvihill, M., *Charlotte Despard*, Pandora, 1989.

89 Pugh, M., *Electoral Reform in War and Peace 1906–18*, Routledge, 1978.

90 Pugh, M., 'The Limits of Liberalism: Liberals and Women's Suffrage 1867–1914', in E. Biagini (ed.), *Citizenship and Community: Liberals, Radicals and Collective Identities in the British Isles, 1865–1931*, Cambridge University Press, 1996.

91 Pugh, M., *The Tories and the People 1880–1935*, Basil Blackwell, 1985.

92 Pugh, M., *Women and the Women's Movement in Britain 1914–1959*, Macmillan, 1992.

93 Pugh, M., *Women's Suffrage in Britain 1867–1928*, The Historical Association, 1980.

94 Raeburn, A., *The Militant Suffragettes*, Michael Joseph, 1973.

95 Ramelson, M., *Petticoat Rebellion: A Century of Struggle for Women's Rights*, Lawrence and Wishart, 1967.

96 Ramsden, J., *The Age of Balfour and Baldwin 1902–1940*, Longman, 1978.

97 Rendall, J., *The Origins of Modern Feminism: Women in Britain, France and the United States, 1780–1860*, Macmillan, 1985.

98 Romero, P., *E. Sylvia Pankhurst: Portrait of a Radical*, Yale University Press, 1987.

99 Rosen, A., *Rise Up, Women! The Militant Campaign of the Women's Social and Political Union 1903–1914*, Routledge, 1974.

100 Rover, C., *Women's Suffrage and Party Politics in Britain, 1866–1914*, Routledge, 1967.

101 Rubinstein, D., *Before the Suffragettes: Women's Emancipation in the 1890s*, Harvester Wheatsheaf, 1986.

102 Rubinstein, D., *A Different World For Women: The Life of Millicent Garrett Fawcett*, Ohio State University Press, 1991.

103 Shanley, M., *Feminism, Marriage and the Law in Victorian England*, Princeton University Press, 1989.

104 Smith, H., 'British Feminism in the 1920s', in H. Smith (ed.), *British Feminism in the Twentieth Century*, Edward Elgar, 1990.

105 Stanley L. and A. Morley, *The Life and Death of Emily Wilding Davison*, The Women's Press, 1988.

106 Stocks, M., *Eleanor Rathbone*, Victor Gollancz, 1949.

107 Strauss, S., *'Traitors to the Masculine Cause': The Men's Campaigns for Women's Rights*, Greenwood, 1982.

108 Sutherland, J., *Mrs. Humphry Ward*, Oxford University Press, 1990.

109 Tanner, D., *Political Change and the Labour Party 1900–1918*, Cambridge University Press, 1990.
110 Tickner, L., *The Spectacle of Women: Imagery of the Suffrage Campaign 1907–14*, Chatto and Windus, 1988.
111 Turner, J., *British Politics and the Great War*, Yale University Press, 1992.
112 Vellacott, J., *From Liberal to Labour with Women's Suffrage: The Story of Catherine Marshall*, McGill-Queen's University Press, 1993.
113 Vicinus, M., *Independent Women: Work and Community for Single Women 1850–1920*, University of Chicago Press, 1985.
114 Walker, L., 'Party Political Women: A Comparative Study of Liberal Women and the Primrose League, 1890–1914', in J. Rendall (ed.), *Equal or Different: Women's Politics 1800–1914*, Basil Blackwell, 1984.
115 Walkowitz, J., *Prostitution and Victorian Society: Women, Class, and the State*, Cambridge University Press, 1980.
116 Wiltsher, A., *Most Dangerous Women: Feminist Peace Campaigners of the Great War*, Pandora, 1985.
117 Winslow, B., *Sylvia Pankhurst*, UCL Press, 1996.

B. Articles

118 Close, D., 'The Collapse of Resistance to Democracy: Conservatives, Adult Suffrage and Second Chamber Reform, 1911–1928', *Historical Journal*, 20, December, 1977.
119 Eustance, C., 'Protests From Behind the Grille: Gender and the Transformation of Parliament, 1867–1918', *Parliamentary History*, 16, No. 1, 1997.
120 Fletcher, I., '"A Star Chamber of the Twentieth Century": Suffragettes, Liberals, and the 1908 "Rush the Commons" Case', *Journal of British Studies*, 35, October, 1996.
121 Hirshfield, C., 'Fractured Faith: Liberal Party Women and the Suffrage Issue in Britain, 1892–1914', *Gender and History, 2,* Summer, 1990.
122 Holton, S., 'The Suffragist and the "Average Woman"', *Women's History Review*, 1, No. 1, 1992.
123 Jarvis, D., 'Mrs. Maggs and Betty: The Conservative Appeal to Women Voters in the 1920s', *Twentieth Century British History, 5,* No. 2, 1994.
124 John, A., '"Run Like Blazes": The Suffragettes and Welshness', *Llafur*, 6, No. 3, 1994.
125 Leneman, L., 'Northern Men and Votes For Women', *History Today*, 41, December, 1991.
126 Mason, F., 'The Newer Eve: The Catholic Women's Suffrage Society in England, 1911–1923', *Catholic Historical Review*, 72, 1986.

127 Mayhall, L., 'Creating the "Suffragette Spirit": British Feminism and the Historical Imagination', *Women's History Review*, 4, No. 3, 1995.

128 Montgomery, F., 'Gender and Suffrage: The Manchester Men's League for Women's Suffrage, 1908–1918', *Bulletin of the John Rylands University Library*, 77, No. 1, 1995.

129 Park, J., 'The British Suffrage Activists of 1913: An Analysis', *Past and Present*, 120, August, 1988.

130 Pugh, M., 'Politicians and the Woman's Vote 1914–1918', *History*, 59, October, 1974.

131 Purvis, J., '"Deeds, Not Words": The Daily Lives of Militant Suffragettes in Edwardian Britain', *Women's Studies International Forum*, 18, No. 2, 1995.

132 Purvis, J., 'A "Pair of ... Infernal Queens?" A Reassessment of the Dominant Representations of Emmeline and Christabel Pankhurst, First Wave Feminists in Edwardian Britain', *Women's History Review*, 5, No. 2, 1996.

133 Purvis, J., 'The Prison Experiences of the Suffragettes in Edwardian Britain', *Women's History Review*, 4, No. 1, 1995.

134 Rasmussen, J., 'Women in Labour: The Flapper Vote and Party System Transformation in Britain', *Electoral Studies*, 3, No. 1, 1984.

135 Smith, H., 'British Women's History: The Fawcett Library's Archival Collections', *Twentieth Century British History*, 2, No. 2, 1991.

136 Smith, H., 'The Politics of Conservative Reform: The Equal Pay for Equal Work Issue, 1945–1955', *Historical Journal*, 35, No. 2, 1992.

137 Smith, H., 'Sex vs. Class: British Feminists and the Labour Movement, 1919–1929', *The Historian* [US], 47, November, 1984.

138 Vellacott, J., 'Anti-War Suffragists', *History*, 62, October, 1977.

139 Vellacott, J., 'Feminist Consciousness and the First World War', *History Workshop Journal*, 23, Spring, 1987.

The Fawcett Library at the London Guildhall University holds the most important collections of archival material relating to the non-militant suffrage campaign. Margaret Barrow and Harold L. Smith have provided guides to this archival material [33, 135].

INDEX

DATE DUE

F 99/	Fout	Reserve	
GAYLORD			PRINTED IN U.S.A.

DATE DUE
